Donald E. Blake
R.K. Carty
Lynda Erickson

Gras.
Party
British Columbia

UBC Press
Vancouver

ISBN 0-7748-0378-9 (cloth)
ISBN 0-7748-0384-3 (paper)

Canadian Cataloguing in Publication Data

Blake, Donald E., 1944–
Grassroots politicians

Includes bibliographical references and index
ISBN 0-7748-0378-9

1. Political activists – British Columbia.
2. Political parties – British Columbia. 3.
British Columbia – Politics and government.
I. Carty, R. Kenneth, 1944–   II. Erickson,
Lynda. III. Title.

JL439.A45B43 1991   324.2711   C90-091765-2

This book has been published with the help of a grant
from the Social Science Federation of Canada, using funds
provided by the Social Sciences and Humanities Research
Council of Canada.

UBC Press
University of British Columbia
6344 Memorial Rd
Vancouver, BC V6T 1Z2
(604) 822-3259

T

1003337184

Contents

Tables and Figures

FIGURES

Preface

This is a book about British Columbia's party politics. In particular it is concerned with the provincial party system though the relationship to the quite different patterns of federal party competition in the province is never far from centre stage. We hope that those concerned to understand the province and its politics will find much food for thought and ammunition for argument in these pages.

At the same time this book is designed to explore the workings of what might be characterized as a model of polarized two-party competition. We have chosen to do this by focusing on party activists, those individuals who populate the party organizations, give them ideological content, and choose and constrain the leadership that carries the partisan battle to the wider electorate. Because our case is a Canadian one, we are also able to discover something of the ways in which party activists simultaneously relate to different party systems operating at distinctive levels of political life. The point of federalism is to make such a politics possible but too many studies assume that nationalizing party politics is necessary to make federalism work.

The political parties' activists are very much at the core of this book and we hope that we have made a contribution to understanding the men and women who stand between the politicians and the electorate. It is their commitment to democratic participation that sustains electoral politics in contemporary liberal democracies. Canadian political science has too often ignored them. By taking these grassroots politicians seriously as critical actors we can learn much about party organization and political competition.

In any large-scale project there are inevitably many people who are involved but whose contributions are really only known and appreciated by the authors. We want to thank them all. Our first obligation is to the more than eight hundred British Columbians who freely choose to participate in our surveys. This book is about them, and the central role they play in the province's politics, and could not have been done without their participation.

We have been helped and counselled by friends, colleagues, and acquaintances at all stages in the research. Rachel and Rob Gourley helped us get started by lending us their house so we could attend the Whistler Social Credit convention. Sharon and Don Carty provided the best of all possible locations for a sabbatical for one of the authors. A Leave Fellowship from the Killam Foundation assisted another. Grant Burnyeat, Kim Campbell, Chris Harris, Jerry Lampert, Greg Lyle, Bill McCarthy, Terry Morley, Vaughan Palmer, Bruce Pollock, Gerry Scott, Joyce Statton, Judy Stevens, and David Stewart all shared their knowledge and experience of provincial parties with us. Few of them are likely to agree with all our views but all have had some part in shaping them.

David Elkins and Richard Spratley at UBC provided invaluable help for the project. Party leadership selection conventions are often sprung with little warning and without their assistance, sometimes beyond the call of duty, the surveys on which this book rests could not have been done. The Social Sciences and Humanities Research Council supported a conference where the analysis in Chapter 7 was first presented. Once the project was launched it might not have been completed without the energy and work of Stephanie Hudson, Nancy Mina, Petula Muller, and Joan Young. Three graduate students assumed most of the responsibility for conducting the Liberal party survey so we owe a special thanks to Michael Mayer, Anthony Sayers, and Robyn So.

Norman Ruff of the University of Victoria, and Anthony Sayers and Robyn So at UBC, made special contributions of data and analysis and this can be seen reflected in Chapters 3, 6, and 9. Two other colleagues deserve our thanks. George Perlin, of Queen's University, got us involved in this sort of work while visiting at UBC and we hope he appreciates the result. André Blais, at the University of Montreal, has been (sort of) patient while we worked on this rather than other projects we are committed to.

This book is unlikely to be the final word on the matters it touches. Earlier versions of some of the analysis can be found in *B.C. Studies* and the *Canadian Journal of Political Science*. The data sets have been deposited in the UBC and Simon Fraser University data libraries and we invite any and all to use them.

GRASSROOTS POLITICIANS

CHAPTER ONE

The Polarization of BC Politics

In its political context the term 'polarization' conveys an image of two opponents who are far apart on most issues having to do with the role of government, the organization of society, and the operation of the economy. In polarized politics there is no centre, or at least the centre is very weak, and contestants for control of government are backed by supporters who occupy positions close to the extremes of the left/right continuum. According to democratic theorists (Dahl 1956:97–8) this situation may lead to instability, assuming the groups at the extremes are numerically balanced, since the compromises necessary to achieve majority decisions would be seen by one side or the other as betraying fundamental principles. Assuming alternation in office, each side would want to undo the handiwork of the other once it managed to achieve power. Active partisans in such a setting would have consistent and coherent sets of political beliefs, and view election campaigns as akin to religious crusades. British Columbia's politics are frequently described as polarized. To what extent do they fit this image?

Left-wing politics got an early start in the province. Parties and organizations ranging from groups of mild reformers to bands of militant socialists appeared in British Columbia at the turn of the century in association with the struggle for the rights of workers and the recognition of trade unions (McCormack 1974). While battles were literally fought and lives were lost in these struggles, it was not until 1933 that the left had sufficient strength to win more than a token presence in the legislature. In that year the Cooperative Commonwealth Federation (CCF) received one-third of the vote and with seven seats (15%) became the official opposition in the BC legislature.

The CCF was a Canada-wide federation of farmer, labour, and

socialist parties, committed rather more to reform than to revolution. However, its BC component contained a much higher proportion of Marxist socialists committed to fundamental change than was true elsewhere (Young 1981). Hence, one could argue that by 1933 the left pole of British Columbia's provincial party system was firmly established.

What about the right? Following the arrival of partisan politics in the provincial legislature in 1903, control of government alternated between the Conservatives and Liberals. There is little evidence of ideological differentiation between those parties or that they sought anything more than to appeal to as many groups in society as possible. Even workers' complaints were recognized by the establishment of minimum wage laws and workers compensation (Dobie 1980 [1938]). When pressed, these traditional party governments did intervene on behalf of capital during such major clashes as the Nanaimo Coal Strike. But on the whole, the 1903-33 period is best characterized as a struggle between 'ins' and 'outs,' rather than right versus left.

That situation changed with the onset of the Great Depression. The incumbent Conservative government led by Simon Fraser Tolmie commissioned a blue-ribbon panel of businessmen to come up with recommendations to deal with the economic disaster. Their plan, calling for massive cuts in government expenditure, reduction of the civil service, and a freeze on welfare rates, was fairly standard in the North American context as the response from the right side of the political spectrum to the crisis. However, the Conservative government (and party) collapsed before the 1933 election and the plan was not adopted.

They were succeeded by the Liberals who, despite the ravages of the Depression, managed to contain the CCF, and, indeed, themselves moved leftward. With massive public works projects, improved welfare programs, and agitation for a national unemployment insurance program, the Pattullo Liberal government placed itself on the progressive side of provincial government responses to economic calamity. Though weakened by electoral defeat in 1933, the provincial Conservative party survived and by 1937 had recovered sufficiently to displace the CCF as the official opposition in the legislature. At the end of the decade, party alignments appeared quite straightforward. The Liberals controlled the centre, facing the CCF on the left and the Conservatives on the right (Robin 1973).

The 1941 provincial election failed to produce a legislative majority for any party and so provided the impetus for a consolidation of the non-left in the form of a governing coalition of Liberals and

Conservatives. On the basis of its legislative program, it would be misleading to call the coalition 'right-wing.' But ten years of coalition government and two elections in which the CCF and coalition were the only real choices produced a new rhetorical phase. The image of left/right polarization began to take hold in the province.

The collapse of the coalition and the subsequent election of a minority Social Credit government in 1952 marked a new stage in the development of polarization (Elkins 1976). Before the decade was out, Social Credit had emerged as the strongest party in the system, the Liberals were reduced to a small rump group in the legislature, and the Conservatives were eliminated altogether. The CCF dominated the opposition ranks, but with a vote share hovering around one-third, it was never a serious threat to challenge Social Credit's hold on government.

Despite the dominance of the party system by Social Credit and the CCF, the left/right cleavage did not completely structure the provincial party space. Both parties also represented a British Columbia variant of populism. In the prairie west, populism had its roots in an agrarian society which, faced with what it took to be economic exploitation of the farming community by the institutions and elites of central Canada, called for greater direct democracy and the decentralization of power to ordinary people as the means to achieve more equitable policies (Laycock 1990). Reflecting these rural origins, glorification of mass action was accompanied by a distrust of modern urban life and the alleged superiority of educated professionals and bureaucrats.

Social Credit owes much of its initial success to financial and organizational support from the Alberta party and electoral support from expatriate Albertans. As a protest movement, however, its attention focused on established provincial political and economic elites and the dominant position of Vancouver as a finance, trade, and service centre. Edwin Black has described it as an 'institutionalized protest against established social elites of all kinds,' whether they be located in the labour movement, the business community, or the universities (Black 1979a:230). None of the three Social Credit premiers had any formal education beyond high school and their cabinets departed considerably from the Canadian pattern in which lawyers and other professionals dominate.

It was also less suspicious of the market economy than prairie populists. In fact, its version of free enterprise emphasized the importance of small business and the dangers of unrestrained big business. Donald Smiley (1962) once described them as Canada's *Poujadists*.

The CCF's populist credentials were of even longer standing. The party's roots are in a tradition with important populist elements to it including a vigorous commitment to democratic control combined with a strong antipathy to centralized bureaucratic institutions such as banks and large corporations. But populist sentiments may have sat more uneasily in the CCF. The party was also committed to cooperative enterprises and it offered a social agenda for the state which required bureaucratic structures and competent professionals to administer.

Whatever the patterns of the 1950s, they have been reshaped by economic development, population growth, and changes in the character of BC socialism. The CCF was transformed into the New Democratic Party (NDP), confirming a shift away from socialism towards social democracy. The NDP also faced more hospitable electoral conditions as the province's economic boom extended the resource economy, with its highly unionized work force, into areas of the province hitherto hostile to the left. Public sector growth increased the number of voters sympathetic to the NDP's economic and social message, especially given the Social Credit government's weak track record on issues such as public sector unionization and teacher salaries. Analysis of election results reveals a slow but steady growth in NDP support across the province beginning in the mid-sixties. Party support became less concentrated in regions where the left had been strong for decades. Increased competitiveness and the temporary disintegration of Social Credit's anti-left coalition, marked by a resurgence in Conservative party support as W.A.C. Bennett failed to provide for his party's renewal, culminated in the 1972 NDP victory (Blake et al. 1981).

Reaction to that victory by the left signalled the final stage in the development of a party system consisting essentially of only two highly antagonistic opponents. William R. Bennett secured the Social Credit party leadership after his father's retirement and immediately began to rebuild the party's mass base. Even unsympathetic observers acknowledge that the effort was a huge success. By 1975, the party had attracted 75,000 members (Palmer 1989b) by playing upon fear of the NDP. An unprecedented scramble for Socred nominations produced well-attended and hotly contested meetings throughout the province (Harris 1987).

Political elites also awakened to a new strategic reality. The 1972 election had returned five Liberals and even two Conservatives to the legislature. However, with NDP support well above its long-term average (and destined to increase even further), it became clear that opponents of the left must unite or else face the prospect of continued NDP victories linked to fragmentation on the right. Several prominent Liberal and Conservative activists announced their intention to join the Social Credit party, and eventually most of the sitting Conservative and Liberal MLAs did so as well (Kristianson 1977). The 1975 election restored a Social Credit government but saw returned only one MLA (a Liberal) from the traditional parties; by 1979 there were none.

Bill Bennett took steps to consolidate the party's hold on the anti-NDP vote and to downplay its populist past. This could have been expected given the younger Bennett's personal style. But it also represented an effort to retain the support of groups such as urban professionals, the mainstay of the Liberals throughout the fifties and sixties, many of whose leaders moved to Social Credit during the realignments of the seventies. The party organization was modernized and placed in the hands of a professional director. Much more effort was expended on fundraising which, at its peak under chief fundraiser Michael Burns, produced nearly $4 million in a single year (Palmer 1989a). Public opinion polling became a regular activity between elections. As we show in Chapter 3, changes in the demographic profile and federal partisan ties of Social Credit party activists between 1973 when Bill Bennett took over the party and 1986 when he retired from public life, reflected these developments.

However, there is some evidence that these efforts actually undermined the mass base of the party. Membership dropped from 75,000 to 33,000 by the time of the 1983 provincial election (Palmer 1989b).[1] We explore disillusionment among party members further in Chapter 8 where we argue that the reaction of the grassroots to this forced party modernization was a factor in the election of William Vander Zalm as leader.

The NDP was slower to modernize, perhaps because its support continued to grow despite defeat in 1975. David Barrett, premier from 1972 to 1975, hung on to his party's leadership (first won in 1969) until 1984. Nevertheless, the party had changed in important ways both before and after its period in government. Table 1 provides striking evidence of the extent to which party candidacies have come to reflect NDP support among public sector professionals and administrators. Although there are some inter-election fluctuations, the proportion of NDP candidates from these occupational groups jumped from under 20 per cent to over 40 per cent between 1966 and 1983. During the same period, the proportion of candidates with blue collar occupations fell from roughly 15 per cent to less than 10. With a strong contingent of candidates from high-status professions (law, medicine, and accountancy) the modern NDP projects a distinctly middle- and upper-middle-class image.

TABLE 1

Occupational background of NDP candidates, 1966–85
(horizontal percentages)

	Private sector professional	Public sector professional	Union/party bureaucracy	Blue collar
1966	10.9	16.4	7.2	14.5
1969	25.5	27.3	0.0	12.7
1972	12.7	21.8	5.5	10.9
1975	16.4	25.5	5.5	7.3
1979	15.8	26.3	3.5	10.5
1983	14.0	45.6	5.3	7.0
1985	10.1	40.6	5.8	5.8

NOTE: percentages do not sum to 100 because not all occupations are represented in the table. Those omitted include clergy, secretarial, clerical, business executives, small business, and housewife. The public sector group consists of public school, college, and university instructors and administrators as well as social work. SOURCE: *BC Statement of Votes* for years indicated.

While, as we show in Chapter 5, the New Democrats' party activists have not abandoned their commitment to social democratic values, there are tensions associated with this development. For instance, the 1984 leadership battle produced a standoff between the followers of long-time MLA Bill King, a former locomotive engineer strongly backed by organized labour, and David Vickers, a lawyer and former deputy minister, whose recent party membership and commitment to socialism was questioned by some. In the end, a coalition of organized labour and more left-wing delegates produced a victory for Robert Skelly. In contrast, his successor, Michael Harcourt, was elected by acclamation at the 1987 NDP convention. Nevertheless, the debate over what kind of left party the NDP should or can be is a continuing one.

POLARIZATION AND GOVERNMENT POLICY

The preceding analysis suggests that 'polarized' may not be a completely accurate description of the party system in the sense that for much of the period from 1933 only the left pole was occupied in any regular coherent fashion: the right was unified only during the coalition period (1941–52) and after 1975. Party rhetoric conveys a different message. Throughout the 1950s, the CCF and Social Credit parties characterized each other using the language of ideological extremes. 'Free Enterprise versus Socialism' was W.A.C. Bennett's favourite election slogan, and there is some evidence that the electorate accepted this description of BC politics (Blake 1985:82). CCFers were similarly convinced that Social Credit was simply a front for powerful capitalists. Both parties portrayed the contest as dangerously close.

An examination of government policy reveals a more complex picture. In the mid-fifties, government spending on education, health, and social welfare was well above the Canadian average, and Social Credit had no ideological qualms about joining the other provinces and the federal government in a massive expansion of shared-cost programs in these areas. However, this eventually changed so that by 1972, the final year of the senior Bennett's administration, only expenditures on health care exceeded the national average (Simeon and Miller 1979).

Nevertheless, Bennett's attitude towards the economy was definitely not laissez-faire (Black 1979a). The government-owned railway became a major instrument for opening up the interior and north to economic development. The premier assumed a major say in the routing of oil and gas pipelines, and created a provincial ferry fleet to replace the private sector as the principal provider of transportation links between the mainland and Vancouver Island as well as along the coast. Perhaps the best example of Social Credit's willingness to interfere with private enterprise is the creation of BC Hydro. The corporation was created after a provincial takeover of BC Electric, the major generator and distributor of electricity in the province (Tomblin 1990). It then proceeded with a massive program of dam and powerline construction to produce fundamental changes in the provincial economy and the distribution of industry. The style with which the Bennett government pursued these and other policies was typical of the action orientation associated with conservative populism. In short, it would be misleading to characterize Social Credit governments before 1972 as simply right-wing.

Nor, notwithstanding the views of some critics, does the label 'socialist' or 'left-wing' adequately describe the NDP government of 1972–5. Some private companies were taken over by the government, but most of them were sold willingly by owners concerned about bankruptcy or unable to justify additional investment in obsolete plants. Government actions in these cases were motivated more by a concern to save jobs than to control, plan, or restructure the economy. The creation of a government monopoly in the auto insurance field is obviously an exception, but the fact the Insurance Corporation of British Columbia has survived for over fifteen years under Social Credit governments suggests it was not particularly offensive to the free enterprise party.

The New Democrats' decision to grant public servants the right to strike was hardly pathbreaking. It had already been taken at the national level and in a number of provinces with Liberal and Conservative governments. The new provincial Labour Code tilted the balance between employer and worker in the latter's favour, but it too survived largely intact until 1987, and was viewed with considerable favour by employers many of whom welcomed the move to restrict the role of the courts in labour disputes.

Certainly initiatives like rent controls, the creation of the office of Rentalsman (the arbiter in landlord and tenant disputes), attempts to involve community groups in the development and administration of social policy, as well as large increases in social spending were unlikely to have been undertaken by a Social Credit government. Nevertheless, they were not particularly radical by Canadian or European standards (Resnick 1977).

Still, the mere fact of an NDP victory was itself a stimulus to the realignment discussed above. Some members of the province's political and economic elite no doubt believed that the government's actions might appear relatively innocuous but actually represented the first step on the road to socialism. Others feared the re-election of the NDP would frighten off potential investors. Finally, after two decades of budget surpluses under Social Credit, the provincial budget failed to balance. Although it was plausible to blame economic recession for the shortfall, the NDP acquired a reputation for economic mismanagement which has dogged it ever since.

Although many NDP initiatives were retained initially by the new (1975) Social Credit government led by Bill Bennett, after the 1983 election a comprehensive restraint program of dismissals, expenditure cuts, program cancellations, and legislative changes was suddenly introduced in the name of economic recovery. This 'restraint program' placed Social Credit squarely in a neo-conservative camp and undoubtedly dramatically increased both the symbolic and real policy distance separating it from the NDP. Arguably for the first time, there seemed to be no question about the existence of polarization. However, the style in which restraint policies were introduced and implemented alienated some of the government's own supporters, as well as large portions of the electorate, and undoubtedly contributed to Bennett's decision to resign rather than face possible election defeat. As we shall see in Chapter 8, Bennett's move to the right was out of phase with the views of many Social Credit activists involved in the choice of his successor.

POLARIZATION AND THE ELECTORATE

Figure 1 provides a graphic illustration of the transformation of the BC party system viewed in terms of electoral support. By 1953, the two big provincial parties shared 75 per cent of the total vote. That grew to 79 per cent with the virtual elimination of the Conservatives from electoral competition in 1966 and to 89 per cent by 1975 following the final stage of the party system's realignment between 1972 and 1975. In the most recent election, nearly 92 per cent voted either Social Credit or NDP.

In most accounts, electoral polarization in modern industrial societies is also associated with class-based voting. The party of the left is usually anchored in the working class, particularly among trade union members, while support for the party of the right is particularly tied to the middle and upper middle classes. We have already cast some doubt on the accuracy of the terms 'left' and 'right' when applied to British Columbia's parties and provincial party competition. Still, there is no doubt that social class is an important determinant of party support in the province. An individual's likelihood of voting Social Credit increases in a strong linear fashion with income, and the NDP leads Social Credit by a substantial margin among blue collar workers (Blake 1985:80).

But voters' ideological positions are not structured exclusively along social class lines. Individualism and collectivism, defined respectively as values which favour personal responsibility for one's own economic well-being and values which support provisions for the collective sharing of risks and benefits, are not entirely coincident with social class. In fact, working class individualism and middle class collectivism are significant determinants of cross-class voting. In 1979, for example, individualistic blue collar workers were twice as likely (63% versus 30%) to vote Social Credit compared to the blue collar group as a whole. Conversely, those in managerial and professional occupations with collectivist sympathies were 1.5 times more likely to vote NDP than the upper status group as a whole (Blake 1985:84).[2]

Nor is a simple left/right dichotomy the only aspect of popular beliefs which affects party support. Working class populism is especially important to Social Credit support (Blake 1984). As we demon-

FIGURE 1
BC provincial vote, 1952–86

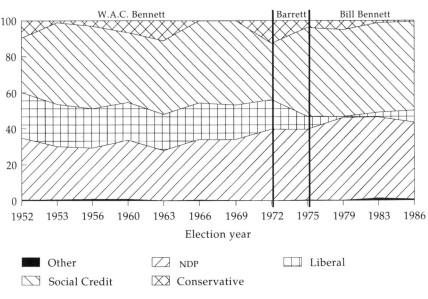

SOURCE: *BC Statement of Votes, 1986*

strate in Chapter 4, populist values have considerable appeal to Social Credit activists as well, and they played a critical role in determining the choice of the new leader in 1986 (Chapter 8).

Finally, the expansion of public sector occupations coupled with the increased salience of size of government issues on the political agenda has added new features to election battles. Whether by accident or design, the Social Credit restraint program launched following the 1983 election, with its message contrasting the privileged position of public sector workers to the suffering inflicted by economic recession on the private sector, created increased tension within the NDP's blue collar constituency. The divide between those in the public and private sectors is beginning to mediate and blunt the class character of British Columbia's electoral alignments.

STUDYING THE PARTIES

Scholars now know a good deal about party history in British Columbia and about the social and ideological underpinnings of support for the two major parties in the modern party system. The policies of Social Credit and NDP governments have also been analyzed in some detail. We have suggested that limited policy differences and cross-class voting qualify the polarization label. Still, perceptions may count for more than statistics on government spending or reviews of government policies for the politically involved.

To understand the pattern of party polarization in British Columbia, and what it means for those who drive the system, we need to examine systematically the values and beliefs of those who constitute the party cores. These are the activists behind the party images, the people who give life to the organizations by choosing party leaders, nominating candidates and working in electoral campaigns. In the NDP, at least, they have a crucial role in determining policy and, in the Social Credit party, help shape the party's direction and governing style by their choice of leader. Among Liberals they are the tiny but determined band who keep the party alive, if only just, in the province. This book is about these party activists in British Columbia. As we shall see, most of them are also very active in national political parties and their partisan activity is one of the major forces that link the otherwise separate provincial and federal political worlds inhabited by British Columbians.

In Canada, we have only just begun to study the men and women who are Canadian political parties' activists. Though George Perlin and his colleagues (1988) have provided portraits of those who take part in the sporadic leadership conventions of national parties we know little about the men and women who make up the parties in the provinces and who keep these political organizations functioning at the grassroots. There are good reasons to begin with party activists in just one province, in this case British Columbia. It is obviously simply easier to conduct research in one system where the activists are close at hand. We are thus able to bring a good deal of contextual information to bear on the analysis, a marked advantage given that this is the first such study in Canada. More importantly, perhaps, a focus on one province allows us to examine party activists across, and within, a coherent provincial party system. As these are the most basic and autonomous organizing units of Canadian party life this seems particularly appropriate. This allows us to examine how the activists see and interpret the competitive system they take part in and consider how that affects their behaviours. Thus we can explore questions such as why individuals stay active in a hopelessly weak party like the provincial BC Liberals, or how New Democrats interpret continuing Social Credit electoral victories.

The next chapter analyzes party activists in general. Who are they, and how do they vary from one party to the next? We also compare them to people active in the national parties and in other provinces to see how typical BC is (or is not).

Chapter 3 compares British Columbians active in politics today with those in the early 1970s to see how they differ. Did the emergence of clear two-party competition lead to a transformation in the parties themselves? We are able to show that contemporary Social Credit activists are better educated, wealthier, and less diverse in terms of ties to the national parties; while the NDP is now considerably more middle-class, white collar, and professional.

The subsequent three chapters are then devoted to an in depth analysis of the values and beliefs of Social Credit, New Democrat, and Liberal activists, respectively. We also compare them to those active in the national parties to answer key questions posed by political observers. For instance, has Social Credit simply become a local branch of the federal Conservatives? Are New Democrats more left-wing than their national counterparts as suggested by the history of the BC party system, or is the party subject to the kinds of divisions which so often plague parties of the left? Are the Liberals really the centre party as they claim, or are they simply a bunch of misfits who do not relate to the central issues of provincial politics?

Chapter 7 focuses on the parties as organizations, looking in some detail at three recent conventions which chose the Social Credit, NDP, and Liberal leaders. By comparing the three parties in action we can say something about their differences but also something about their similarities and show how the delegate selection process affects the kind of leader chosen.

Chapter 8 is then devoted exclusively to the choice of William Vander Zalm as Social Credit leader in 1986. With Social Credit in power, participants were choosing the premier, not just a party leader. Moreover, with twelve candidates, the battle for succession was the most contested leadership struggle in Canadian history. Our analysis explores the fissures in the party this contest opened up and shows how grassroots party members can actively work to transform their own party. In this case, Social Crediters deliberately repudiated the leadership of Bill Bennett with the choice of a populist outsider to succeed him.

We then shift the analysis to the level of the party system and examine the question of Liberal survival in Chapter 9. During the last two decades, the provincial Conservative party has folded its tent and disappeared. Not so the Liberals. Why? What keeps these people active in a party that has no chance? In answering this question we explore some of the links between federal and provincial political activity. We also come to grips with the idea of the centre in a polarized two-party system.

The final chapter gives us the opportunity to reflect on the characteristics of the provincial party system from the perspective of spatial theory. With only two parties left in active contention they ought to resist polarization and mirror one another as they both approach the centre in search of support. But this does not seem to have happened: the parties have retained substantial elements of difference and the system is still not balanced. Social Credit nearly always wins and has been in power for all but three years for some four decades. As our British Columbia case illustrates, party militants do carry distinctive subcultures and these appear to have a significant impact on the ongoing dynamics and immediate outcomes in competitive party systems. Thus we start our analysis of the party system with a look at the parties' activists.

CHAPTER TWO

Party Activists in British Columbia

Political parties in British Columbia, like those in other provinces as well as the national arena, commonly appear to be driven and dominated by the elected politicians who make up their legislative caucus. And of all these figures the parliamentary leader generally stands head and shoulders above his or her colleagues. Indeed the distinctive and obvious prominence of party leaders in Canada was remarked upon by foreign observers as early as the turn of the century (Siegfried 1970 [1906]). The invention of leadership selection conventions early in this century, first in the provinces and then nationally, only reinforced this unique dimension of Canadian party organization and life. Not surprisingly then, when we think about parties we often instinctively cast them in terms of their leaders and their professional politicians.

At the same time it is almost impossible to talk about parties without talking about the great divides in Canadian social and economic life. Thus parties are portrayed as the representatives of the English or the French, of farmers or workers, of Westerners or central Canadians, of Catholics or Protestants, or more likely some complex shifting coalition of particular groups. But this is to speak of parties in terms of their electoral supporters, rather than as organizations with a institutional life of their own.

The gap between politician and voter is often wide. Political parties exist to bridge it; they were first organized in the nineteenth and twentieth centuries to provide some permanent link between the two, and to give that link coherence and meaning. Modern British Columbian political parties enroll thousands of members and it is these individuals – the party activists – organized in constituency associations and ancillary groups, and meeting regularly in convention, that give the parties life, shape, and permanence.

Despite all the forms and trappings of internal democracy, parties in Canada are relatively oligarchic organizations dominated by a small number of politicians who decide most questions of policy and strategy, and direct its day-to-day affairs. Although a party's many activists are rarely engaged in high politics it would be an error to ignore them or their activities. They have three vital roles to play. First, it is the ordinary party members who constitute the working body of any electoral organization. Parties exist to elect members to the legislature and this requires people working in every constituency to maintain and run an organization at election time. These activists recruit supporters, canvass voters, raise funds, oversee polling stations, and perform the vast array of other tasks common to an election campaign. Even with modern party campaigns organized and run by paid professionals, without some network of local activists a party has little chance of victory.

Party activists' second major contribution is to define the organization as a community of believers. No matter how fuzzy and ill-defined, or how ideologically sharp a party's stance may be, it requires a body of activists to carry its ideas, its traditions, and its commitments. These attitudes and beliefs are what give a party its own identity and purpose, that give it some permanence across time as activists pass the organization on to new generations. This is not to say that a party's politicians always faithfully represent the ideas that define their parties, or that these systems of ideas are unambiguous and unanimously held in a party. But parties cannot be understood independently of their activists' beliefs and leaders stray from the bounds they define at their peril.

Finally, the third thing activists do is to decide and to choose. At local meetings and in provincial conventions activists vote on questions of party organization and policy, they nominate candidates for office and they select party leaders. In these last two the activists go a long way to putting their stamp on the parties' caucuses and political leadership. Thus, even if politicians have considerable leeway in determining policy, the activists can apply the brakes or accelerate the rate of change by changing the politicians who speak for them. For instance, Social Credit activists could alter the style of their government by replacing Bill Bennett with Bill Vander Zalm; the province's New Democrats could reach for the centre ground by selecting the moderate Mike Harcourt as leader and surrounding him with a caucus of middle-class professionals.

Our appreciation of the important role played by party activists leads us to ask three basic sets of questions. First, what sorts of people join political parties? Do they have long histories of activism or fleeting commitments? Second, to what extent do parties gather like minded individuals together? How do the attitudes and preferences of activists define a party, shape its policies, and constrain its leaders. Third, and finally, how do these activists go about the important task of deciding and choosing? What factors influence their decisions as to whom to support for positions of influence and leadership? Are the internal politics of parties about the clash of ideas or do they stem from more traditional interests and personal factors bumping up against one another? And through all of these sets of important questions we shall be looking for the signs of continuity and change that are simultaneously part of the life of modern political party organizations.

To obtain our profiles of the party's activists we chose to focus our attention on those who attended provincial leadership conventions. We selected these conventions because of the special place they have in Canadian parties and because of the opportunities they provide to observe the inner soul and workings of the respective organizations. Leadership conventions, which symbolize the determination of party activists to hold their elected leadership and parliamentary representatives accountable to the membership, are viewed as the most vital and exciting party activity. As such, there are often vigorous local contests to become delegates, and elaborate personal campaigns for the leadership. Canadian parties are always aware that a new leader often means new directions and so the selection process inevitably involves considerations about future policy. Both these features guarantee that, more than other party conventions and meetings, the keenest, most influential, and most involved activists will attend when the leadership is at issue. By focusing on these conventions we can tap into the core of the party at a time when it is most concerned to define its future, and when open contests allow us the clearest look into the otherwise rather closed world of a party's organization.

THE BRITISH COLUMBIA ACTIVIST STUDIES

To answer our many questions about party activists we conducted surveys of all the delegates to recent leadership selection conventions in British Columbia's two major and one minor party. Fortunately for our purposes, all three met to choose a new leader within fourteen months of one another in 1986-7 so that the party system context of these conventions was basically similar. Social Credit met first, in the summer of 1986, in a highly contested convention to choose a leader and premier to succeed Bill Bennett. Bill Vander Zalm won and so for the first time in Social Credit history party members entrusted the leadership to someone other than a member of the Bennett family. Vander Zalm promptly called and won a fall 1986 election setting the stage for New Democratic and Liberal party leadership conventions. As it happened both of those post-defeat conventions went uncontested. In the spring of 1987, the New Democrats, who had survived a hard fought leadership battle just three years previously, quietly agreed on Mike Harcourt, a newly elected member of the legislative assembly and former Vancouver mayor. A few months later, in October, the provincial Liberals acclaimed Gordon Wilson, a relatively unknown college instructor, their new leader.

To maximize comparability, the surveys of each of the parties were as similar as possible. We asked members of all three parties a common set of questions about political attitudes as well as their policy perceptions and preferences. We also asked identical questions about these party activists' political experience and partisan activity. Finally, we asked all our respondents a wide range of questions about their own socio-economic backgrounds and social involvement. These questions allow us to compare and contrast activists within and between the three parties. At the same time each of the questionnaires had a series of questions about the leadership campaigns and conventions that the respective delegates were engaged in. Naturally enough, the very different contests and convention structures meant that these portions of the surveys varied considerably from one party to the next. Nevertheless, even here there is considerable material for comparison. What these surveys tell us about party activists is the subject of the chapters that follow. In the next, we are able to paint a portrait of what sort of individuals are party activists in British Columbia and, using data collected by Norman Ruff in the mid-1970s, demonstrate the changing composition of the organizations. The section that follows moves to a consideration of the attitudes and beliefs of the three parties' activists and we look at each in turn to build a profile of the ideational patterns of party competition in the province. That analysis is supplemented and strengthened with data on activists in national party organizations which allows us to compare the federal and provincial levels political life as well as situate British Columbia activists within the wider national spectrum.

We then move to our third set of questions which are concerned with how activists go about choosing and deciding. In these chapters, we move from a broad cross-party comparison to a close examination of the competitive dynamic within the governing party in some detail. Then, in the final pair of chapters, the data allow us to explore questions of continuity and change. First we ask why the Liberal party persists despite a decade of electoral disasters. Why have their activists resisted being absorbed into Social Credit or the New Democrats? This leads to comparison of the two principal parties in terms of the systemic and structural limits to change and convergence as well as the images of polarization. Inevitably, we are brought back to the activists, their ideas of politics and the parties they build and sustain.

The surveys which provide these rich data sources were all completed by the delegates immediately after the respective conventions and mailed back at their discretion. In the case of Social Credit, delegate lists were obtained from the campaign organizations of several of the leadership candidates and questionnaires were mailed to delegates from all but one of the constituencies. (One constituency was missed because of an incomplete list but this does not appear to distort our findings in any way.) The survey, the first of its kind in British Columbia, rapidly became a matter of conversation amongst party activists. Some telephoned the authors about it, seeking copies of the results (which were made freely available), others apparently complained to the party office about the invasion of their privacy. After some discussion with the authors about its appropriateness, the Social Credit party president Hope Wotherspoon wrote a brief letter to all the delegates informing them that the project had not been sanctioned by the party executive and recommending that members ignore it. By that time however the vast bulk of the returns were already in and returns had begun to dwindle. At that point, a few were returned blank but an equal number, accompanied by the President's letter, were completed and returned with a note indicating that no one told Social Credit party members what to do.

This experience, coupled with more planning time, led us to solicit more formal party cooperation for the New Democratic and Liberal convention surveys. In both cases party officials agreed to support the project and the questionnaires were accompanied by an endorsement: from the provincial secretary of the NDP and from the party president of the Liberals. The New Democratic questionnaires were mailed to all registered delegates after the convention while in the Liberal case they were personally distributed at the time of registration. And it may be that this official recommendation made some difference, for return rates were higher in both the New Democratic and Liberal parties.

For these three parties convention size varied with both the size of the party membership and the extent to which the leadership was contested. Thus both the Social Credit and New Democratic conventions were considerably larger than the Liberals', but the New Democrats had fewer activists attend than were eligible (774 of 1078) or had been at their 1984 convention when the leadership had been fought for by six candidates. Thus our surveys produced differing numbers of responses (Table 2).

TABLE 2
Return rates from delegate surveys

	Delegates surveyed	Responses	Return rate (%)
Social Credit	1275	340	27
New Democrat	774	373	48
Liberal	240	90	40

With such differences in both the survey process and the response rate we were concerned to ensure that each sample was representative of the delegates at the respective conventions. In each case we are confident they are. For Social Credit this was a potential problem given the smaller response rate and the apparent controversy over the survey itself. But for this party we have six separate indicators – gender, region of residence, and four distinct leadership ballots – by which we can compare the survey respondents with the convention delegates as a whole. On each one they matched. In the case of the New Democrats only two variables – region and delegate category – provided a direct check but again the match was very close. Almost half the New Democrats told us they had been at the leadership convention held only three years previously and they reported a vote pattern that corresponded to those results. That suggests NDP conventions do not change very quickly. Finally, the Liberal respondents also match the larger convention in terms of region and delegate category.

With over eight hundred respondents we have a large sample of British Columbia's most active and involved party members. From them we can learn much about the shape and content of party organization and politics in the province, and the linkages between federal and provincial party activity. Though we shall have a good deal to say about these men and women throughout this book it is worth stopping for a moment at this point to draw a sketch of just who they are.

THE PARTIES' ACTIVISTS

It should come as no surprise to any observer of Canadian parties to learn that these British Columbia conventions are dominated by middle-aged, well-educated, relatively affluent males. This has certainly been the case in the national parties (Perlin 1988) and seems also to be true in other provinces. Recent attempts to increase the number of women delegates have not been particularly successful and still only about one-third are female though the larger numbers at the 1990 national Liberal party leadership convention suggest gender quotas do make a difference. Later chapters provide detailed profiles of the three parties' activists on these and other dimensions.

There is an especially important aspect which distinguishes these delegates from those at national party conventions and this relates to what we might describe as their anthropology. These conventions are dominated, to a far greater extent than the national ones, by the established working core of the local constituency organizations. Curiously, this is the reverse of what one might expect: national parties have room for far fewer delegates from any single constituency and one might assume that local leaders would be the obvious local choices.

We can see this when we compare the local constituency association delegates to the 1983 Progressive Conservative and 1984 Liberal national leadership conventions to our British Columbia party delegates. When asked whether they felt 'part of or close to' the establishment in their (national) party only 9 per cent of the Conservative and 13 per cent of the Liberals answered yes. But when we asked the delegates to the provincial Social Credit and NDP leadership conventions whether they thought of themselves as part of the party's 'central group' in their constituency, fully three-quarters said yes. While these are somewhat different questions they testify to both the flavour of this difference we are talking about and to the more institutionalized character of provincial conventions.

On reflection these patterns make political sense. Given the geography of the country, it is almost inevitable that most activists would feel more removed from the centres of influence in national as opposed to provincial party organizations. It is also likely true that vigorous leadership campaign constituency contests (Carty 1988) for relatively fewer delegate positions in national parties produce a more random assortment of activists at those conventions.

These differences also reflect an organizational reality. The provincial parties are dominated by activists who have a long and varied record of partisan service. Thus over half the delegates in all three provincial parties were serving (or had served in the past) on their local constituency executive. Over three-quarters (almost 90 per cent in the NDP) reported that they had raised money for the party. Ninety per cent had worked actively in a local candidate's campaign organization, and two-thirds had been at previous provincial (or national) party conventions. Given these records, it is not surprising that some two-thirds of these partisans had been party members for over a decade. In contrast, among national party constituency delegates a good 10 per cent fewer had been party members that long.

There is another related way in which party activists at the two levels seem to differ. In both the national party samples, a considerable majority of delegates thought the party depended too much on professional organizers who weakened the role of ordinary party members. In all three provincial parties the delegates overwhelmingly disagreed with that proposition (although they did think there was too much emphasis on polling). This we take as further evidence of a greater sense of confidence and more organizational involvement and power that provincial level partisans have.

Provincial parties can thus perhaps be best described as more intimate than their national counterparts. Geography alone would predict that more activists would know and interact with fellow partisans in other areas but their extensive experience and service ensures that conventions are almost like family reunions. Indeed the analogy may not be too far-fetched for our provincial convention data indicates that, in each of the three parties, as many as a quarter of the delegates were related to one another. Decision-making in this forum is bound to vary somewhat from the chaotic hurly-burly of national party conventions.

This brings us back to our central set of questions. How do these people think about politics? How do they decide on such vital questions as their party's leadership? What are the dynamics for change in a party system with such apparently stable groups of partisans? We begin to answer these questions in the next chapter by first looking at the extent to which the parties' activists have changed over the decade that marked the final polarization of party competition in British Columbia.

CHAPTER THREE

Continuity and Change:
Party Activists, 1973–87

NORMAN RUFF WITH THE AUTHORS

Political parties are inevitably institutions of both continuity and change. They bear memories of battles fought, definitions of old issues still to be settled, and traditions that shape the careers and options of contemporary politicians. At the same time, they must continue to absorb and reflect the changing patterns of a dynamic society and economy. It is the tension between these two impulses that shapes parties' organization and activity.

Individual party members and activists carry these traditions and mirror social changes. Thus we can observe in the shifting profiles of a party's activists the balance between continuity and change as well as the party's response to the changing competitive environment and its place in it. In this chapter, we use this technique to examine how, if at all, the Social Credit, New Democratic and Liberal parties in British Columbia have changed over the last decade with the emergence of a polarized two-party system.

The leadership convention studies of 1986 and 1987 provide a good deal of information about the contemporary parties. Fortunately, we also have some parallel information on a number of important dimensions similarly gathered at provincial party conventions in the early 1970s. Survey data from the Social Credit leadership convention which choose Bill Bennett in 1973, and from the NDP and Liberal party conventions of 1973 and 1974, respectively, allow us to compare the three parties at the beginning and end of the Bill Bennett era. In the case of the NDP it is also possible to extend some of the analysis back another decade using Walter Young's study (Young 1971) of the party in the mid-1960s.

The data we have provide portraits of the parties from three perspectives. First, it is possible to examine socio-economic profiles of the parties' activists searching for any changes among them or over time. Second, we can consider their levels of partisan involvement as one measure of the organizational life and coherence of the party. Finally, it is possible to say something about the nature of federal-provincial partisan ties and the extent to which party members in British Columbia inhabit different political worlds, one focused on Ottawa and the other on Victoria.

For all the political turbulence and partisan conflict of the Bennett-Barrett years in British Columbia we do not expect to see dramatic changes in the composition of party organizations. A decade and a half is not a particularly long time in the life of a political party and continuities in the strategic setting and terms of debate in the BC party system after the 1972 to 1975 realignment surely outweigh the changes in those years. But there is a second reason to expect to find limited change. A party's core of activists is rather stable with those entering or leaving making up a small proportion of the total membership in a given period. Thus they will likely be slower to reflect social changes than will the party's professional politicians who must cope directly with a less committed and potentially more volatile electorate.

Perhaps the most obvious structural change in the BC party system in the decade after 1972 was the creation of genuinely bipolar two-party competition. The Liberal party disappeared from the legislature and its share of the vote in provincial elections shrank to about 5 per cent. However, the party, as an organization, continued to persist and it may be that there is now some distinctive cast to those that choose to remain active in this semi-moribund party.

The New Democrats moved from being a party that regularly commanded about one-third of the vote to one that has the support of just under half the electorate. One might expect some of these new supporters to be active now in the party. As a consequence, the NDP should have a somewhat more socially heterogeneous core of activists than when it represented a more narrowly defined interest in the province. We expect Social Credit, which maintained its position as the province's governing party over the period, to have changed the least.

PROFILE OF THE ACTIVISTS

An examination of the basic socio-economic profiles of the three parties' activists in the early 1970s and then the mid-1980s confirms our basic expectation that continuity rather than change would be the dominant pattern. This is summarized in Table 3 which provides data on a series of different dimensions. Not only is there evidence of limited change but where there are differences they are principally of degree rather than kind. The most dramatic change has been the growth in the number of activists with higher education, especially amongst New Democrats. However, on this variable like most of the others, the rank order of the three parties has not changed.

TABLE 3
Demographic profile of party activists
(percentages, 1966–87)

| | Social Credit | | New Democrat | | | Liberal | |
	1973	1986	1966	1973	1987	1974	1987
Male	64.2	69.3	70.0	61.4	66.3	53.0	66.3
Over 55 years	33.1	35.7		17.6	25.4	18.2	42.5
BC-born	33.3	42.6		40.9	43.0	37.5	37.5
>15 years resident		87.7			81.3		82.0
RELIGION							
none	6.7	18.5	47.0	47.6	55.8	20.9	27.1
Catholic	10.0	12.4	7.0	7.2	7.3	18.2	21.2
United/Anglican	48.5	31.6	26.0	25.3	18.4	46.7	29.4
other	34.8	37.5	20.0	19.9	18.5	14.2	22.3
University-educated	17.3	28.7	25.0	20.3	46.1	34.3	61.4
Self-employed		50.6			12.1		24.7
High income	23.0	42.3		7.5	28.9	33.0	38.7
MEMBERSHIPS/INVOLVE- MENT							
trade union	17.0	8.7	34.0	47.1	47.9	21.5	13.2
professional association	11.6	56.2		5.1	39.1	20.6	70.7
ethnic group		14.1			9.9		14.3

NOTE: The 'high income' category in 1973 was over $20,000; in 1986 it was over $50,000.

It is also evident that more than ever before the party activists in British Columbia look like a socio-economic elite. With higher educations and incomes than in previous years, and with a much increased proportion claiming to be members of a professional organization of some kind, these provincial activists clearly now look like the societal elites that dominate national party conventions. The numbers of trade unionists active in provincial party life seems to have declined overall: though they just held their own in the NDP, where they make up half the activists, the numbers have dropped in both the Liberal and Social Credit cases to the point where they can have little impact in those parties.

Whatever losses the Liberals have suffered among ordinary British Columbians they still find champions in the upper middle classes. A larger proportion of Liberals are professionals and have a university education than is true in the other parties, though more Social Credit activists now appear to be in the highest income group than do Liberals. This is one marked change from the early 1970s. It appears to be largely a function of the comparatively high numbers of self-employed entrepreneurs in Social Credit: its activists' education levels still remain lower than either of the other two parties.

These modest shifts in the character of Social Credit activists reflect its coming of age as a governing party. Though it retains many of the forms and attitudes of a populist movement, the party's active core is now dominated by the economically privileged interests of the society. Bill Bennett's determination to transform the old-fashioned, populist Social Credit organization he inherited into a professional, modern, right-of-centre party appears to have been remarkably successful.

Liberal activists do appear to be older. There is no doubt that convention rules, timing, and location have a greater impact on the proportion of young people and students able to attend a party convention than is true for other age groups. But given that the 1974 Liberal convention was in Vernon, while the 1987 one was in Vancouver, one would assume that the latter would have been more accessible to young people and Liberal campus clubs organizations. Yet our data reveal a striking increase in the proportion of Liberal activists over fifty-five years of age between the two conventions. This suggests that politically interested young British Columbians may be responding to the Liberal party's provincial electoral decline by not joining the party. If that is the case it could disappear as a viable organization when these older Liberals leave the political stage. But, as we shall see below, the story is rather more complicated than simply that of a party literally dying.

New Democrats, as we hypothesized, do look rather more middle-class, and hence heterogeneous, in the mid-1980s than they did in the early 1970s or the 1960s. This is clearly reflected in the significant increase in university-educated activists. The proportion doubled over the most recent period (having been stable in the previous decade) so that now half the NDP activists are university people.

With this change has come an increase in the numbers in the highest income group – over a quarter now have annual family incomes of over fifty thousand dollars – and there has been a big jump in the proportion reporting professional association memberships. With a more heterogeneous and middle class core of activists the NDP will find it difficult to sustain the argument that class naturally orders political conflict.

In several other obvious ways neither the parties nor BC political life seems to have changed very much. Despite the fact that the province continues to receive large numbers of immigrants from other parts of Canada as well as other countries, most activists are long-time residents. In light of the province's social and racial pluralism, surprisingly few report involvement in ethnic groups. This leads us to conclude that the parties are likely to reflect the prejudices and instincts of the dominant majority community. New groups and new approaches to politics brought from outside the province are not likely to find an easy reception in the party system.

Nowhere is this so apparent as in the virtually unchanged proportions of women attending party conventions. The years in question have seen women's issues, and the role of women in the political system, high on the Canadian and provincial political agendas. Virtually all parties have passed resolutions supporting increased participation by women in party and electoral life. Most have begun to try to make good on them. The New Democrats made formal commitments to gender equality in party office and the Social Credit organization was presided over by a woman at the time of our study. Yet none of these significant developments are reflected in the gender balance at these recent party conventions. British Columbia's extra-parliamentary parties remain predominantly male-dominated institutions.

Religion, which marks so much of Canadian politics, has never been regarded as an important dimension of political competition in British Columbia. Yet for all that there remain some traditional differences among the three parties. The New Democrats are the party of 'no religion.' Half of their activists decline to offer any religious identification, even of the most nominal sort. Liberal partisans are predominantly drawn from the country's three largest Christian churches (Roman Catholic, United, and Anglican) and, like the party in most of the rest of the country, the BC party is more Catholic than its opponents. Social Credit activists are far more likely to identify a religious affiliation, with the largest single group coming from the three big churches.

Though the province's party balance changed considerably during the years of the Barrett and Bennett governments it seems that the parties themselves did not. Slow to change, the parties are dominated by partisans with deep loyalties and long-standing commitments.

PARTISANS AND LOYALISTS

The men and (fewer) women who are at the heart of the BC parties have little doubt about their politics. And they appear to have had relatively little doubt in the past. In the early-1970s, when asked if they had ever 'felt closer' to another party, fewer than one in five said yes. For the New Democrats the proportion was even smaller – just 8 per cent. Some fifteen years later the question we asked party convention delegates referred to whether they had ever 'been active' in another party and the percentage of affirmative answers was sharply lower. Again the New Democrats were the least likely ever to have had a different political home. Less than 5 per cent admitted to it (Table 4).

TABLE 4

Level of partisan involvement
(percentages)

	Social Credit		New Democrat			Liberal	
	1973	1986	1966	1973	1987	1974	1987
Involved in other party							
'closer to'	20.0			7.7		14.4	
'active in'		7.4			4.3		6.7
Member >5 years	57.0	69.2	56.0	57.5	63.0	59.0	56.7
Attended previous convention	45.6	66.8	70.0	71.9	70.2	63.8	59.1
At previous leadership convention		18.2			44.2		47.8

Two aspects of the partisanship of these activists are worth noting. First, it seems stronger amongst New Democrats. This is not surprising and is what one might expect given the important role of ideology in defining and holding together a party that has spent virtually all of the past half-century in opposition. Another way of thinking about this would be to suggest that those with previous different political attachments are less likely to make it into the

organizational core of the NDP and be chosen as convention delegates. Again, this is what one might expect in a more ideologically
oriented opposition party.

The second aspect of this phenomenon to note is that the parties
generally do not appear to recruit key activists from among former
opponents. This is not necessarily what one would expect from
catch-all brokerage parties like the Liberals or Social Credit. Their
success is dependent upon winning over individuals from any and
all perspectives, including the enemy camp. If they do so, such
individuals are not being effectively integrated into their organization. This seems most obvious with respect to former Liberals. Given
the widespread shrinkage of that party, there must be significant
numbers of former Liberal activists now voting for the NDP or Social
Credit. But they must also have dropped out of active political life
for they are not showing up at provincial conventions of the two
major parties.

Table 4 also shows that the long-term commitment of activists
described in Chapter 2 is a continuing phenomenon in these parties.
Indeed in the case of Social Credit and the NDP, the number who had
been members for more than five years increased in the 1980s. At the
same time we discovered that a fairly large proportion (43%) of the
Liberals had joined over the past half decade. Clearly then the party
is not merely a cadre of slowly aging Liberals incapable of attracting
new members and so doomed to die with its last activist.

As men and women with considerable histories of partisan experience, these delegates were not newcomers to party conventions.
Very large proportions of all three reported attending previous
party conventions. Given that the convention is the central institution of the extra-parliamentary party organization, this suggests
that it has an ongoing existence. These activists, who come again
and again, give the party conventions a coherence, continuity, and
autonomy needed to ensure that they have a presence in the life of
the party. Conventions like these, dominated by experienced activists, will inevitably act as constraints on the leadership.

Almost half the delegates to the 1987 New Democratic and Liberal
leadership conventions reported being at their party's previous provincial leadership convention. In Social Credit almost one in five had
been, which seems rather remarkable given the thirteen year gap
between the two meetings. This suggests a degree of accountability
in the leadership selection process that certainly does not exist in the
national parties. At the federal level, party leadership conventions
dominated by one-time delegates of uncertain political background
look more like political happenings than aspects of a sophisticated

institutional process. Our record of the BC parties over time suggests that there is more, rather than less, to them than meets the eye.

FEDERAL-PROVINCIAL ORGANIZATIONAL LINKS

British Columbians exist in two political worlds. The federal world is inhabited by Conservatives, Liberals, and New Democrats; the provincial one largely by Social Crediters and New Democrats. Not only are these worlds asymmetrical but the overlap is neither clear nor predictable. There are far more provincial New Democrats than federal voters of the same persuasion, and federal Liberal supporters obviously divide into various groups for provincial elections. In subsequent chapters, we explore some of the ideological overlap and crosscurrents, here we can say something of the organizational loyalties of the activists and chart recent changes.

Voters may live in a bifurcated political world but activists, especially with the enduring partisanship that we have seen characterize these BC party members, do not. Their commitments hold across both levels of political life, albeit in an unusual way for Social Credit, making this group of British Columbians central actors in the effort to tie together federal and provincial political activity within the province. Table 5 reveals the federal party orientations of the three sets of activists in the two decades.

TABLE 5
Federal ties of provincial activists
(vertical percentages)

	Social Credit		New Democrat		Liberal	
	1973	1986	1973	1987	1974	1987
Federal orientation						
Social Credit	41.9	0.0	0.0	0.0	0.0	0.0
New Democrat	0.4	0.9	99.0	98.6	0.0	2.3
Liberal	11.6	6.0	0.3	0.3	99.2	94.3
Progressive Conservative	38.1	91.3	0.0	0.9	0.4	2.3
other	8.0	1.8	0.7	0.3	0.4	1.1

NOTE: figures for 1973 based on party identification; for 1986 and 1987 on reported vote in the 1984 federal election.

Unfortunately the data are not strictly comparable. In the 1970s, those attending the provincial conventions were asked for their party identification in federal politics. In the 1980s, the relevant question asked how they voted in the previous (1984) federal general election. A question about vote might have produced different results among Socreds in 1973, whereas the scale of the Conservative landslide in 1984 may have somewhat altered the typical Socred pattern in 1986. Even keeping these limitations in mind, the data provides a striking portrait.

There is virtually no leakage of New Democratic or Liberal provincial party activists to other parties in federal politics. And this is a reality of those parties' organizational life that has not changed at all over the period. Despite the uncertain electoral fortunes of the Liberals in BC – and in the 1984 federal election they were extraordinarily low – activists kept these two parties tightly tied together.

Social Credit was different. In the 1970s, large numbers of its activists claimed allegiance to the federal Social Credit party despite the fact that it was then little more than an eccentric remnant of a never very strong federal party. Given that the federal party in BC was generally seen as a temporary creation of then-premier W.A.C. Bennett it may be that those provincial activists actually constituted the bulk of federal Social Credit supporters. But whatever the case, Social Credit activists in the 1970s had a variety of federal political links. Fewer than 40 per cent were Conservatives, despite Bennett's Tory background, making the party a real coalition of the many federal partisan interests in the province.

By 1986 that had dramatically changed. Social Credit activists were now clearly as politically homogeneous as either of their opponents: over 90 per cent of them were federal Progressive Conservatives. The party itself is no longer a coalition of distinct federal forces but an organizational mirror image of British Columbia's Tories. Though the two organizations maintain a formal distance, relations are probably better and closer than between some parties of the same partisan complexion in other provinces (e.g., Liberals in Quebec). Federal Conservative leaders have implicitly recognized this linkage across levels in their relations with their own provincial party counterpart. Although it maintains a formal existence as a provincial organization, in the last two elections the Progressive Conservative party of British Columbia ran fewer than fifteen candidates for a fifty-seven-member house. Yet federal leaders have done virtually nothing to assist the party.

In this environment we find politicians and key party strategists easily move back and forth between the federal Tories and Social Credit, public acknowledgement of the overwhelmingly Conservative cast of the modern Social Credit party. For example, Kim Campbell, a Conservative MP and cabinet minister, began her political career in Bill Bennett's office, sought the provincial leadership, and was elected to the legislature as a Social Credit MLA in 1986 before jumping to the federal arena. Bob Wenman sat as a Social Credit MLA before election as a Conservative MP, and then, after years in Ottawa, returned to run as a Social Credit leadership candidate in 1986. High-profile party professionals such as Jerry Lampert and Pat Kinsella have served the Conservative party in Ontario and Ottawa as well as Social Credit in BC.

The other side of this Social Credit coin is the fact that the proportion of federal Liberals in the party is now half what is was in the early 1970s. This despite the fact that Bill Bennett attracted several one-time Liberal MLAS (including a former provincial leader) into his caucus and cabinet. These individuals played prominent roles in Social Credit governments for a decade but obviously were not able to carry significant numbers of their active supporters with them into the Social Credit party.

This analysis demonstrates that, by and large, party activists in BC do not live in two political worlds. Theirs is one tightly integrated federal-provincial political existence. For Social Credit activists, the name changes to Progressive Conservative for federal politics but otherwise they do not look so different from the New Democrats on this dimension.

The Liberals in our group are something more of a puzzle. As a party they face a difficult political environment across both levels of politics in BC, but their electoral fortunes are particularly dismal in provincial politics. At the federal level their support amongst the BC electorate dropped from an average of 33 per cent of the popular vote in the 1960s to 20 per cent in the 1980s as the West in general and BC in particular became disenchanted with the party under Trudeau and failed to be attracted back under Turner's leadership. As a result, the party went from being competitive in a three-way race with the Tories and the NDP to running a poor third. But its fifth of the vote province-wide in federal elections seems respectable, even in the 1980s, compared to its provincial showing (see Figure 1). Yet a number of highly educated individuals stay active in the provincial party. Why they do so is dealt with more extensively in a later chapter, but Table 6, which compares Liberals and New Democrats, provides a hint. Provincial Liberal activists clearly see the federal political world as more important than do New Democrats. Given that our activists were attending a provincial leadership selection convention this Liberal predisposition towards federal politics is striking. They may be primarily oriented towards BC's federal politi-

cal world, participating in provincial politics simply as a consequence of their federal involvement.

TABLE 6
Relative importance of political arena
for New Democrats and Liberals
(vertical percentages)

	New Democrat	Liberal
Level of politics most important		
federal	39.9	77.2
provincial	60.1	22.7

If this analysis demonstrates that party activists in BC live in a
coherent and well-integrated political world, we know the same is
not true for the electorate. And this phenomenon of one political
world for the activists, two for the voters, is the source of considerable misunderstanding even within the parties. Two-thirds of the
New Democratic activists, when asked about the quarter of their
provincial electorate that does not support them federally, say that
those provincial supporters vote Liberal in federal elections. On the
other hand, when we asked the Liberals who all the federal Liberal
voters support in provincial elections, half believe that they go
straight to Social Credit, most of the rest suggest that the federal
vote splits in various other ways (but basically favouring Social
Credit), and only 2 per cent think they vote NDP. Obviously one,
or perhaps both, of these groups of provincial activists must be
wrong. While survey data might tell us which, the important point
here is that the provincial party activists do not have a clear, shared
understanding of the political worlds of their voters. This incongru-
ence between the political world of activist and voter cannot help
the parties deal realistically with the competitive environment of BC
politics.

CONCLUSION

This analysis of party activists has allowed us to escape for a
moment the static portrait that survey evidence so often provides.
Looking at the three parties over two decades largely confirms what
we expected but in ways that allow us to highlight important
dimensions of the development of the party system.

In particular, it is clear that the NDP is becoming a more heterogeneous and typically social democratic party. Its activists are more middle class and better educated than those in the governing free enterprise party. In large part this probably reflects the growing allegiance of the professional public sector to the NDP noted in Chapter 1. In the process, the party is being slowly transformed. It appears that Bob Skelly, leader from 1984 to 1986, may go down as the last gift of the traditional trade unionists to the party while Mike Harcourt's 1986 leadership victory represents the ascendancy of these new groups within the NDP.

Social Credit looks like a party of the province's elites in a way that it certainly did not at the end of W.A.C. Bennett's years as leader. This is a transformation that was probably inevitable as it finally consolidated the anti-socialist vote under one partisan banner. Curiously, in doing so the party has apparently become less of a genuine coalition and more of a provincial version of the national Conservative party. That is not what one would have expected to happen when it finally managed to swallow up most of the province's Liberal elites.

Finally our analysis points to sharp differences between the political worlds of the party activists and the electorate. It is difficult to speculate about all the consequences of this divergence but we believe that this can be quite dysfunctional for the parties. We return to this important theme in the last chapter.

CHAPTER FOUR

Social Credit: Pragmatic Coalition or Ideological Right?

The Social Credit party faces a complex political environment. It is an organization which claims to represent one pole in a simple bipolar party system. Yet it also claims to represent a diverse, free enterprise coalition of supporters of major federal parties in provincial politics. This Janus-like character inevitably leads to internal tension and raises a number of questions with respect to the structure of opinion within the party, not the least of which concern party cohesiveness and ideological ties with the major federal parties. In this chapter we consider these issues as we explore the dimensions of ideology and opinion structure among our Social Credit activists.

MEASURING IDEOLOGY

In the survey research literature, the term ideology has been given a variety of meanings. Some scholars reserve the term for opinions on issues that are structured in the sense of being correlated with one another (Converse 1964; Rapoport 1986). Others use the term to refer to opinions on issues which relate to class interests, including issues such as labour rights, social welfare and government regulation (Ornstein and Stevenson 1984). Still others simply use the term to refer to aggregates of opinion in terms of a left-right continuum whether the issues are directly relevant to class interests or not (Blake et al. 1988).

In this study, we use the term ideology in a comprehensive sense because we think it useful to examine attitudes that relate to both class and other left-right issues, and because we think it important as well to look at the patterns of relationships among policy attitudes. Thus we have used a combination of issues and methods by which to study ideology within the party. First, to give us a preliminary picture of the distribution of opinion in the party, we simply calculated the percentages of respondents agreeing with our various question items. Then, to determine the level of consensus within the party, we measured the degree to which our respondents agreed or disagreed with one another on these items. Next we used factor analysis to assist us in creating a number of scales by which to characterize, in more general terms, the opinions of our delegates. Factor analysis is a statistical technique which can be used to reduce a large number of questions to a few clusters of inter-related questions. It is a method which can then help to sort out whether questionnaire items appropriately fit together as measures of a common disposition. The results of factor analyses were also used to suggest whether certain main themes directed issue responses within different categories of delegates and, if so, whether these differ between groups, especially between Social Crediters who support different federal parties.

To measure ideology among Social Credit party activists we directed our questions to a variety of current political issues, including free trade, foreign investment, economic development, social policy, government regulation and the provincial government's wide-ranging restraint program. We also asked more abstract questions regarding individual responsibility and the role and competence of government, as well as some items designed to tap populist sentiment. The attitude scales we formed from the responses included several which have been used effectively to map the structure of opinion in the British Columbia electorate (Blake 1985). Details of scale construction can be found in the Appendix. They are also described in the text as we introduce them into the analysis.

THE IDEOLOGY OF SOCIAL CREDIT ACTIVISTS

The characteristics of Social Credit and the environment of British Columbia politics suggest contradictory hypotheses with respect to the structure of opinion among Social Credit partisans. On the one hand, given the rhetorical polarization between the province's major parties, the suspicion and hostility characterizing the debate between government and opposition in the legislature (NDP leader Dave Barrett was literally dragged from the chamber during the restraint debate after being expelled by the Deputy Speaker), and the attempt by the party leadership to articulate a consistent neo-conservative philosophy following the 1983 provincial election, one might expect Social Credit party activists to exhibit a coherent set of policy views, anchored by commitment to a free enterprise ideology. This expectation is reinforced by the fact that provincial parties in British Columbia are unlikely to attract adherents on the basis of their appeal to aggrieved regional, religious, or cultural minorities – a phenomenon which has muted the left-right distinctions between federal Liberals and Conservatives. Aggrieved religious and cultural minorities are simply not large or self-conscious enough in British Columbia to challenge successfully the ideological definition brought to mass politics by Social Credit and the NDP.

On the other hand, there is ample evidence that many Social Credit voters support the party simply because of their opposition to socialism or the NDP, and not because they are attracted to Social Credit ideology in any positive fashion or because they share any other common political attitudes (Blake 1984:32–5). This could also be true for activists. Given its dominant position, the party now effectively monopolizes provincial career opportunities for the politically ambitious who are not New Democrats.

Analysis of the policy and opinion items we developed reveals a party united on some dimensions, sharply divided on others. Somewhat surprisingly, activists have conflicting views on a number of key social and economic issues which should distinguish their party from the NDP. On others, they are virtually unanimous. This assessment is based on the analysis reported in Table 7. The first column in the table contains the percentage of activists who agree with each of the statements listed on the left. These have been abbreviated for reasons of space, but the full text of each question can be found in the Appendix. The items concern a variety of policy domains – trade policy, economic development, social policy, and the size and role of government – as well as questions designed to tap populist sentiments.

In order to assess the degree of consensus within the party on a given item and to compare across items, a consensus index was created based on the percentage of activists who are on the same side of a given issue. These figures appear in the second column of the table. The index has a maximum possible value of 50 which would be reached if everyone agreed (or disagreed). A 50/50 split would yield a score of 0.[1]

During the leadership campaign which preceded the convention our delegates attended, the major contenders to succeed Bill Bennett went out of their way to avoid endorsing the ideological cast he had given government policy which led to the 1983 battle over restraint (Magnusson et al. 1984; Allen and Rosenbluth 1986). These leader-

TABLE 7
Policy consensus among Social Credit activists

	Per cent agree	Consensus index
Don't spend tax dollars on sick	6.0	44.0
Should have freer trade with U.S.	92.9	42.9
Unions are too powerful	91.7	41.7
People should rely on selves not government	91.2	41.2
Cut red tape in government	90.2	40.2
Government should help women	13.8	36.2
Government should negotiate native land claims	14.2	35.8
Foreign ownership threatens independence	17.3	32.7
Government should guarantee standard of living	24.6	25.4
Reduce size of government	72.0	22.0
The community should support seniors	28.1	21.9
Many welfare programs are unnecessary	68.0	18.0
Government should favour BC companies for contracts	34.3	15.7
Government regulation stifles initiative	64.1	14.1
Should trust down-to-earth thinking	61.0	11.0
Grassroots could solve problems better	57.2	7.2
Preserve independence even at cost of cut in standard of living	44.4	5.6
There should be a law requiring balanced budget	44.5	5.5
Unemployed could find jobs if they really wanted to	54.9	4.9
Restraint program was not well implemented	51.2	1.2

NOTE: The consensus index can range from 50 (completely united) to 0 (completely split). For exact question wording see the Appendix.

ship candidates were (at least retrospectively) ambivalent about a program whose implementation, if not its design, was clearly unpopular with much of the electorate. It appears this ambivalence was shared by the party. The sharpest division in opinion among our delegates occurs over the government's implementation of the restraint program. When asked about why it had encountered such intense opposition, 42 per cent said its opponents were simply individuals who could not accept having lost the 1983 election, but over half the party believed their own government was responsible for not having handled it at all well.

Social Credit activists are very enthusiastic about freer trade with the United States while the social policy role for government elicits

rather different degrees of consensus. There is considerable difference of opinion as to whether the unemployed are responsible for
their plight. And despite their conservative politics, a large majority
endorse tax-supported medical care when faced with the choice
between that and requiring individuals to set aside money to cope
with medical emergencies themselves.

While at this point no clear pattern of consensus within policy
domains emerges, our data do convey the impression that Social
Credit activists have quite heterogeneous responses to several important issues. That impression is reinforced when we examine their
priorities regarding government spending. A detailed comparative
party breakdown of responses is presented in Table 20 below, so only
a brief summary is offered here. Very few are prepared to counte-
nance cuts in government spending for reforestation, highways, tourism, and health care. In fact, over 80 per cent favour an increase in
spending on reforestation, over half would increase tourism spending, and nearly half support increased job creation grants. Most of
our Socred respondents support the status quo on spending in the
remaining areas, but there is a significant minority in the party which
favours cuts in the areas of daycare, social welfare, and government
salaries. The pattern here seems clearer – spending linked to economic development and support for the private sector enjoys considerable support: social spending and public sector support are much
more contentious. Bill Bennett's government with its enthusiasm for
mega-projects was clearly in tune with party opinion on economic
questions. It was perhaps less so on the social side where the government appeared keener to cut than the majority of its activists.

In addition to the questions on various policy issues outlined
above, we presented the Social Credit activists with a series of
options on the regulatory activities of the government (see Table 19
below). It is difficult to provide a simple summary of the views on
regulatory matters, given the fact that respondents could express
varying degrees of support for tighter or looser regulation or indicate support for the status quo. However, the most divisive appear
to be land use regulation, marketing of agricultural products, sale of
alcohol, and gambling. Since an NDP government act of 1973, all land
in British Columbia has been classified according to its suitability for
agriculture. In order to remove land from the Agricultural Land
Reserve for commercial or residential development, which normally
increases its value substantially, permission must be obtained from
a regulatory agency, the BC Land Commission. Since its decisions
can be appealed to Cabinet, the appeal process frequently leads to
political battles. Generally, this form of regulation is criticized by

those involved in property development and real estate – strong supporters of Social Credit. Somewhat surprisingly, only 54 per cent of the party favoured less regulation. Twenty-three per cent favoured the status quo on land use regulation and 32 per cent favoured more regulation. Only 9 per cent approved of the current level of regulation governing agricultural marketing which gives a prominent role to marketing boards for the establishment of prices and production quotas and is perceived to be biased in favour of producers as well as restricting entry into certain branches of the industry. Nearly 58 per cent favoured what is presumably the free enterprise position on the issue – a reduction in regulations. However, a substantial minority, 33 per cent, favoured more regulation.

All this evidence indicates that there is clearly variation among the opinions of activists, but to what extent is it structured by major dimensions underlying political conflict in BC? Table 8 provides a measure of the basic opinion dimensions that provide some order to individual differences on specific policy questions. Using a combination of items in Table 7 and the questions on government spending and regulation, we were able to isolate and identify five dimensions: continentalism, collective versus individual responsibility, populism, opinions on the Social Credit restraint program, and attitudes toward government regulation. Table 8 is organized by decreasing degree of consensus, where consensus is measured by the coefficient of variation (cv in the table). This is simply the standard deviation of a distribution divided by its mean. The smaller the coefficient, the less variation (ie, the more consensus) that exists among Social Credit activists on the relevant dimension. They are most agreed on a pro-continentalist stance, least agreed in their general views towards the extent and range of government regulation.

TABLE 8
Attitudinal variation among Social Credit activists
by issue domain

Attitude scale	mean	Standard deviation	Coefficient of variation	N
Continentalism	2.31	.72	.31	256
Collective v. individual responsibility	3.74	1.19	.32	240
Populism	2.34	.89	.38	253
Pro-restraint	3.23	1.88	.58	248
Anti-regulation	2.75	1.80	.65	318

Support for freer trade with the United States and lack of concern for the perils of foreign ownership characterize those with high scores on the continentalism scale. Cohesion might have been even higher were it not for a significant minority in the party who endorse the proposition that Canada must maintain her independence even if it means a lower standard of living. At the time of the survey, the Social Credit government was a stalwart defender of the federal government's free trade initiative with the United States. Given the number in the party (44.4%) who claim to be prepared to accept a cut in living standards in order to preserve Canada's independence, the basis for consensus on free trade within the party may be somewhat vulnerable. The Free Trade Agreement has also had a major negative impact on the wine grape growing industry in the Okanagan Valley, an area of Social Credit strength. Agricultural marketing boards which favour producers – another group with strong ties to Social Credit – have also come under attack by proponents of freer trade.

The collective versus individual responsibility scale contains six items dealing with the degree to which individuals or the community should take responsibility for the well-being of individuals who are unemployed, ill, or elderly, and whether individuals need to be protected by the state from the consequences of unrestrained free enterprise. The questions used to create this scale tap issues which have been a source of conflict between parties of the left and right. Hence it offers a measure of left versus right polarization at the attitudinal level. The arithmetic mean of the scale is 2.62. Although the mean score of the delegates is weighted to the individualist (high) end of the scale, there is some range of opinion on these matters of public policy.

Like individualist orientations, populist sentiments are widely shared but not universal. Our data show that party activists generally live up to their reputation for hostility to bureaucracy, suspicion of experts, and faith in grassroots opinion. As we shall see, variation on this dimension plays an important part in the internal dynamics of the party. It was one of the principal factors which helped to account for divisions among Social Credit activists in the struggle for the party leadership.

The pro-restraint scale combines several items which may appear to be analytically distinct – downsizing, balancing the provincial budget, spending on public service salaries, education, and welfare, protection for human rights, and general position on the restraint program – but all touch on aspects of the restraint battle which divided the province during 1983 and 1984. Moreover, factor analysis reveals that the items included in this battery all load on the same underlying dimension. Using the three scales above as benchmarks, we find even more variation of opinion on this dimension.

Finally, as with the restraint scale, the regulatory scale taps opinion about what may seem to be diverse issues. But despite the greater moral content of views on alcohol and gambling compared to those regarding other objects of government regulation, there was no evidence from the factor analysis that they constituted a separate dimension. Accordingly, the anti-regulation scale was created using all the items mentioned. As Table 8 suggests, this dimension, like restraint, is one on which the delegates were not widely agreed.

It is clear, then, that differences of opinion do exist within the relatively conservative Social Credit party. However, some domains are more divisive than others. It is noteworthy that partisans seem to be rather more cohesive on our collective versus individual responsibility scale, which we believe taps an underlying left/right dimension, and on populism, than on the restraint and regulation scales. This is not surprising since the latter are associated with concrete policy decisions rather than more abstract ideological principles. However, although the spread of opinion is greater in some cases than in others, all five dimensions point to the existence of differences within the activist group.

Social Credit emerged originally as a party of the province's interior. Following the change of leadership in 1973 and the election of 1975, it grew stronger in the Vancouver metropolitan area. It seems natural, then, to explore the possibility that there is a regional basis to these differences – especially between the interior of the province and the lower mainland. Only one of the dimensions in Table 8 shows any sign of regional variation. That dimension is populism. Modernization of the party and its growth beyond its strongholds in the interior has not eradicated these differences. Activists from the southern and northern interior were significantly more populist than those from the lower mainland with mean scores of 2.42 and 2.58, respectively, compared to 2.09 for the lower mainland. The mean score on populism for Vancouver Island activists was almost exactly the same as the mean for the whole group, 2.33. Further analysis showed that these regional differences are linked to lower levels of education and income in the interior. However, the absence of regional differences on other dimensions, especially collective versus individual responsibility, suggests that adherence to Social Credit ideology has the power to unite activists across regions.

In the next section, we see whether these opinion differences are related to partisan divisions in national politics. Does the Social

Credit party represent an ideological coalition of the federal Liberal and Conservative parties?

LIBERALS AND CONSERVATIVES IN THE
SOCIAL CREDIT PARTY

As noted in Chapter 1, the Social Credit party first came into office in 1952 in the wake of the collapse of a decade-old Liberal-Conservative coalition government. The party, under W.A.C. Bennett, soon usurped the position of the coalition as the free enterprise alternative and, building its own organization largely on the ruins of Conservative provincial constituency organizations, eliminated the Tories from effective competition for government office. But, notwithstanding their more general success in supplanting the coalition as the governing alternative, Social Credit was never fully successful in eliminating the Liberal party from provincial competition. It retained an average vote share of over 20 per cent throughout the 1950s and 1960s. (See Figure 1 above.)

Little is known about Social Credit activists during W.A.C. Bennett's tenure as leader except that the party's annual meetings attracted a curious mixture of religious fundamentalists, funny money Socreds, and right-to-work advocates much to the delight of columnists and editorial cartoonists. This was the period in which the party's constitution pledged them to objectives such as fostering Christian relationships, studying the principles of Social Credit, and liberating the country from the grip of its financial system. Our profile in Chapter 3 captures Social Credit at the very end of that two-decade period. Policy resolutions were either ignored or derailed by the leadership, and Bennett's dominance of the party was never threatened. Moreover, it has been argued that he played a pivotal role in securing the party leadership for his son, Bill Bennett, when he stepped down following the 1972 electoral defeat (Mitchell 1983:435-7).

When Bill Bennett effectively completed the job of consolidating the opposition to the NDP into a single party, he and the party organization managed to convince most prominent provincial Liberals and Conservatives, inside and outside the legislature, to join Social Credit (Harris 1987; Kristianson 1977). In the 1975 election, of the fifty-five Social Credit nominees for the legislature, seventeen (ten Liberals and seven Conservatives) had been incumbents or well-known supporters of the other two provincial opposition parties before the election (Harris 1987: Appendix E). This includes, of course, Bill Bennett's successor, William Vander Zalm.

We can only speculate about what effect these changes had on the ideological mixture among party activists. These high-profile Liberal recruits seemingly outnumbered Conservative ones in Bill Bennett's rebuilt Social Credit party: there were four well-known Liberal politicians but only one Conservative in his first cabinet. Yet his father's pre-1972 party had been built on a large number of supporters with previous affiliations with the provincial Conservative party, many of whom presumably retained ties to their national counterpart. Given this, one might expect Tory perspectives, if distinctive, to predominate.

If the pattern of elite differences is anything like that which exists among voters we would also expect to find post-1972 Liberal recruits to be, disproportionately, strategic Socreds attracted to the party because of their distaste for socialism of the NDP variety and not because of the attractiveness of Social Credit as a policy vehicle (Blake 1985:32–4).

This group must have been somewhat troubled by the cast given to government policy by Bill Bennett following the 1983 election. The restraint program announced in July 1983 continued a wage freeze for public employees, set about reducing the number of civil servants by 25 per cent while simultaneously shrinking public sector bargaining rights, reduced protection for tenants, restricted the scope of human rights guarantees, eliminated a number of social programs, and limited the budgetary authority of local school boards (Magnusson et al. 1984). For the first time, Social Credit seemed to be offering a set of radical policy alternatives informed by an aggressive neo-conservative ideology, albeit with some continuation of the welfare state, rather than simply promising competent management of the province's affairs.

To consider the consequences of this policy shift for the coalitional character of Social Credit, we start by asking about the role of the federal Liberals in the party. Despite the prominence of former Liberals on the Social Credit front bench in the legislature, federal Liberals constitute a tiny minority among Social Credit activists. Only 6 per cent of them voted Liberal in the 1984 election. Membership in federal parties is similarly skewed. Sixty per cent of Social Credit activists acknowledged membership in a federal party, but virtually all of them (93%) are federal Conservatives. Although we have no information on the federal partisanship or voting patterns of the Social Credit party membership as a whole, even given the vagaries of the delegate selection process, it is difficult to believe that the figures would be dramatically different. Some Social Credit activists, especially those with no federal party membership, may have once supported the federal Liberal party, but if they did it seems most of them are no longer voting for it.

TABLE 9
Attitude differences among Social Credit activists
by 1984 federal vote

Attitude scale	Conservative	Liberal	Sig. level
Continentalism	2.33	2.19	.44
Individual v. collective responsibility	3.81	3.18	.04
Populism	2.38	1.75	.01
Anti-regulation	2.35	1.95	.02
Pro-restraint	2.73	1.57	.01

NOTE: Table entries are mean scores. A higher score indicates a position closer to that indicated by the name of the scale. For details see the Appendix. Ns vary by scale because of varying amounts of missing data, but there are approximately 20 Liberals and 300 Conservatives in this table.

However small, the federal Liberal minority does constitute a distinctive group within the Social Credit party on several policy dimensions. Looking at Table 9 and comparing Liberal Socreds with their Conservative counterparts, we find the Liberals are less individualistic, less populist, less hostile to government regulation and more critical of the 1983 restraint program. Only on the continentalism index was there no significant difference between the two groups. While these differing orientations provide a possible basis for detaching these Liberal Socreds from the provincial party, political events transpired to bind them together. The federal 1988 Liberal campaign was run on an anti-continentalist theme, the one issue most likely to help reinforce the pro-free trade Social Credit coalition.

Liberal Socreds differed from the other activists in several further respects: they were more likely (65–55%) to agree that 'the party has to be careful not to move too far to the right' and they were less likely (55–70%) to have supported the populist Vander Zalm on the final ballot for the leadership. This last result is rather ironic given the fact that Vander Zalm started his career as a Liberal, and Brian Smith, his opponent on the final ballot, had well-known federal Conservative ties. This does suggest that differing orientations, at least to tactical and strategic questions, constitute a source of strain within the party.

There seems little doubt then that the Social Credit organization is dominated by those with Conservative Party federal preferences. However, even amongst activists, strategic Socreds exist. Given their antipathy to the NDP and the weakness of the provincial Liberal party, this minority of federal Liberal supporters see no alternative home in provincial politics, but they are not as enthusiastic about conservative positions on social and economic issues as most of their fellow Social Credit partisans.

PROVINCIAL SOCREDS AND FEDERAL ACTIVISTS

Given the small proportion of Liberals among Socred activists, the proposition that the Social Credit party is the provincial counterpart of the national Conservative Party must be taken seriously. Yet while this would lead us to expect that Socred activists are closer to the national Tories than to the national Liberals, the stronger brokerage pressures in the national arena suggest that the national Tory party is likely to be less homogeneous and less distinctive in left/right terms than is Social Credit. This tendency may be reinforced by the differing vantage points of the two levels of government the parties seek to control. For federal activists their vantage point may introduce a geographical or jurisdictional frame of reference that supersedes a left/right one. For example, environmental regulation often raises issues concerned with federal-provincial cooperation, interregional accommodation and Canadian/American negotiations. At the provincial level, however, environmental protection legislation is more likely to pose more direct trade-offs with economic development, particularly in British Columbia which depends heavily on the exploitation of its natural resources. Thus for provincial activists more than federal ones, environmental issues may tend to pit the left against supporters of immediate commercial exploitation.

To compare the Social Credit party with the federal Liberal and Conservative parties we use data from studies of two national leadership conventions, held by the Liberals in 1984 and the Conservatives in 1983.[2] The comparisons between provincial and national (those from all across the country as well as those from just BC) party activists are more limited than is the full analysis of provincial Social Credit activists because of the smaller number of questions (ten) that were asked of all three parties. Consequently, most of our cross-party comparisons use single items. We do, however, use factor analysis to look for signs of differences, between the parties and across levels, in the degree to which opinions are structured by a left/right dimension. That analysis provides support for the construction of a 'continentalism index' and a three-item 'social spending' index which we can then use to compare the intra-party differences and inter-party overlap.

TABLE 10
Attitudinal distributions among provincial Social Credit and federal Conservative and Liberal activists
(vertical percentages)

	Liberal	Conservative	Social Credit
Environmental protection regulation			
increase	77.1	63.5	23.3
decrease	3.0	6.2	30.9
Education spending*			
increase	71.4	55.1	30.9
decrease	3.5	10.5	13.5
Agricultural marketing regulation			
increase	30.6	19.2	42.7
decrease	29.5	54.8	56.2
Welfare spending*			
increase	48.5	32.3	15.0
decrease	6.1	21.8	36.2
Ensure independence	58.1	33.3	42.9
Daycare spending			
increase	59.7	33.8	17.3
decrease	12.9	31.3	55.8
Free trade with U.S.	63.9	80.0	92.4
Unnecessary welfare programs	26.3	64.5	67.4
Job grants to business			
increase	54.6	47.9	44.4
decrease	17.6	30.4	23.8
Independence threatened by foreign ownership	51.5	27.3	17.1

*The education spending question for federal activists specified post-secondary education. The welfare spending question in the Social Credit questionnaire referred to welfare rates; that for national Liberal and Conservative delegates to direct relief payments to the poor. These results are based on 337 Socreds, 926 Conservatives, and 1290 Liberals.

Table 10 records the distribution of answers from Social Credit, and the nationwide samples of Liberal and Conservative delegates on our ten comparable questions, and Table 11 contains the results of a systematic comparison of the three groups using a difference index. The index is calculated by summing the absolute differences between the parties in the percentages falling into each response category and then dividing by 200. It is arithmetically equivalent to the proportion of a given group who would have to change their opinion in order to make two distributions of responses identical. For example, the difference score of 0.40 on environmental protection (Table 11) means that a shift by 40 per cent of the Socreds or 40 per cent of the Conservatives from one category of answer to another would eliminate the differences between them. The index attains its minimum value of 0 when two distributions are identical and its maximum value of 1 when the distributions do not have a single populated category in common.

TABLE 11

Attitudinal differences between provincial Social Credit and federal Conservative and Liberal activists

	Difference score		
Issue	Conservative versus Socred	Liberal versus Socred	Conservative versus Liberal
Environmental protection	.40	.53	.19
Education spending	.23	.40	.16
Agricultural marketing	.17	.39	.25
Welfare spending	.17	.33	.16
Ensure independence	.16	.08	.22
Daycare spending	.16	.42	.26
Freer trade with U.S.	.14	.32	.19
Unnecessary welfare programs	.09	.44	.36
Job grants to business	.09	.11	.13
Independence threatened by foreign ownership	.08	.30	.23
MEAN	.17	.33	.22

NOTE: The larger the difference score, the greater the difference between parties. Also see notes to Table 10.

As expected, the Social Credit activists share the right side of the political spectrum with delegates to the 1983 Conservative leadership convention. Moreover, although there are some exceptions, on most questions the Socreds as a group are located to the right of the federal Conservatives and thus even rather further from the federal Liberals.

The sharpest differences between the Socreds and the other two parties are found in the area of environmental protection, where 77 per cent of the Liberals and 64 per cent of the Conservatives would like to see some extension (slight or substantial) in governmental regulation. The same is true for only 23 per cent of Socreds. The next largest differences are to be found regarding educational spending (difference scores of 0.40 and 0.23) with 71 per cent of Liberals, 55 per cent of Tories, and only 31 per cent of Socreds favouring increased spending. However, some of the differences on this question may be partly an artifact of the differences in wording noted on Table 10.

Welfare spending, daycare spending, and attitudes to free trade show a similar pattern but with smaller differences between the Socreds and Conservatives. The agricultural marketing issue shows much the same pattern, although Social Crediters are more sharply polarized on this question than are the other two parties, with 56 per cent favouring decreased regulation while 43 per cent favour increased regulation. On job creation grants, views on foreign ownership, and in their criticisms of welfare programs, the Socreds and Conservatives converge even more but remain to the right of the Liberals. On only one question were the Socreds closer to the Liberals with 43 per cent and 58 per cent respectively agreeing that Canada's independence must be preserved even at the cost of a lower standard of living. Only 28.7 per cent of the Tories agreed with that statement.

These differences in the attitude patterns among activists in the three parties contain no major surprises. We expect that some of it is a consequence of the more heterogeneous nature of the regional accommodation necessarily practised by Canadian national parties. We can obtain some measure of this by comparing Social Credit activists to just the British Columbia sub-group within each of the national parties.

The spatial arrangement of the three parties on the left/right spectrum remains the same but it is accompanied by a sharp reduction in the magnitude of the differences between activists at the two levels of politics (see Table 12). In particular, comparing Social Credit activists to the BC Conservatives leads to difference scores for education, welfare, and daycare spending of 0.15, 0.05, and 0.08 respectively compared to 0.23, 0.17, and 0.16 for all Conservative activists (Table 12 versus Table 11). Freer trade with the U.S. produces a difference score of only 0.07 (compared to 0.14) and concern about foreign ownership produces a difference score of only 0.01 (as opposed to 0.08). Only on the question of willingness to make economic sacrifices in order to preserve independence are BC Socreds closer to Conservatives as a whole than to the BC delegation.

TABLE 12

Attitudinal differences between provincial Social Credit and federal Conservative and Liberal activists from BC

| | Difference score | | |
| | Conservative versus Socred | Liberal versus Socred | Conservative versus Liberal |
Issue			
Environmental protection	.16	.24	.08
Education spending	.15	.18	.08
Agricultural marketing	.14	.16	.26
Welfare spending	.05	.20	.18
Ensure independence	.23	.14	.37
Daycare spending	.08	.25	.25
Freer trade with U.S.	.07	.22	.15
Unnecessary welfare programs	.05	.50	.49
Job grants to business	.10	.03	.13
Independence threatened by foreign ownership	.01	.34	.34
MEAN	.09	.23	.23

NOTE: these results are based on a total of 337 Socreds, 93 Conservatives, and 149 Liberals. Also see notes to tables 10 and 11.

The gap between the attitudes of Socreds and federal Liberals is also systematically reduced when we look only at those Liberals from the province. But the figures still confirm our argument that even BC Liberals as a group would not sit easily in the Social Credit party. Substantial differences remain on welfare and daycare spending, criticism of welfare programs, and attitudes towards freer trade and foreign ownership.

Given these differences in the centres of gravity among activists in the parties, we might also expect to find some differences in the structure of opinion underlying these attitudes, in particular with respect to the impact of federalism on the definition of issues. However, our attempts to find such differences using factor analysis were not particularly successful.[3]

As we noted earlier, factor analysis is used to identify groups of attitude items which are associated with a smaller set of dimensions (or factors) which appear to structure opinion. The first factor identified by this technique links all the spending items, the assertion about unnecessary welfare programs, environmental regulation, and the marketing of agricultural products. In other words, these items have stronger correlations (factor loadings) with the first factor than the questions on foreign ownership, freer trade, and ensuring Canada's independence. The content of the items with high loadings suggests that responses are structured by an underlying left/right dimension (Table 13).

TABLE 13
Factor analysis of activist opinion
(loading on principal component)

	Socred	All PC	BC PC	All Liberal	BC Liberal
Environmental protection	.48	.50	.20	.56	.62
Education spending	.56	.45	.33	.55	.56
Agricultural marketing	.47	.59	.31	.32	.42
Welfare spending	.55	.58	.67	.58	.56
Ensure independence	.11	.39	.36	.31	.43
Daycare spending	.68	.58	.55	.61	.61
Freer trade with U.S.	−.18	−.39	−.50	−.31	−.17
Unnecessary welfare programs	−.60	−.50	−.33	−.48	−.52
Job grants to business	.60	.49	.57	.40	.47
Independence threatened by foreign ownership	.26	.45	.26	.42	.53
Per cent common variance explained by factor	23.6	24.0	18.8	21.9	25.5

NOTE: Given the coding of responses, the signs of the factor loadings are consistent with the presumed right-wing position on all the issues, ie, a preference for cuts rather than increases in spending on education, welfare, daycare, and job grants; a preference for deregulation in the areas of environmental protection and agricultural marketing; support for freer trade and rejection of the belief that independence is threatened by foreign ownership and that Canada's independence must be preserved at all costs; and agreement with the position that there are many unnecessary welfare programs. Also see notes to Tables 10 and 11.

The remaining items, all dealing in one way or another with Canada's relations with the U.S. are less strongly correlated with the principal component. However, for each group they were related to a second factor which we labelled 'continentalism.'[4]

The percentage of common variance, a measure of explanatory power accounted for by the left/right factor, does not seem to vary much by party except that British Columbians active in the national Conservative convention had relatively low loadings on four of the relevant items. This is consistent with the hypothesis that federalism may affect the federal and provincial parties differently but, given that the direction of the loadings on these items even among Conservatives from BC is consistent with those among other party activists, they are a weak exception to the more general pattern of no differences associated with participation in the different worlds of federal and provincial politics.

The results of the factor analysis justify combining six of the items into two simple additive scales. Details of scale construction can be found in the Appendix. These scales allow us to portray graphically the similarities and differences among activists at the two levels. The first scale, labelled 'continentalism,' combines responses to three items dealing with freer trade, foreign ownership and the preservation of Canada's independence (Figure 2). The second, a 'social spending' scale, combines responses to three questions regarding welfare, education, and daycare (Figure 3).

These graphs illustrate in a simple but direct fashion the basic pattern that emerged in the analysis above. There are very small differences on the continentalism dimension between Social Crediters and Conservatives, whether we take into account all Conservatives or only those from British Columbia. Higher scores indicate stronger support for the continentalist position. Thus the Liberals are least continentalist with a mean score of 1.53 for BC Liberals and all Liberals compared to scores of 2.45 for BC Tories, 2.31 for Social Crediters, and 2.24 for all Conservatives.

A plurality of each of the five groups expresses support for freer trade with the U.S., rejects the notion that foreign ownership threatens Canadian independence, and is unwilling to sacrifice living standards to preserve independence. The differences which do emerge are largely the result of the last item. Only 29 per cent of federal Conservatives were willing to pay the price of independence compared to 43 per cent of the Socreds. For the latter this question seems linked to their populist sentiments and it may not be perceived by many of them as being tied to the other economic issues associated with continentalism. While different from the Social Credit and Conservative partisans, BC Liberals are virtually indistinguishable from Liberal activists as a group.

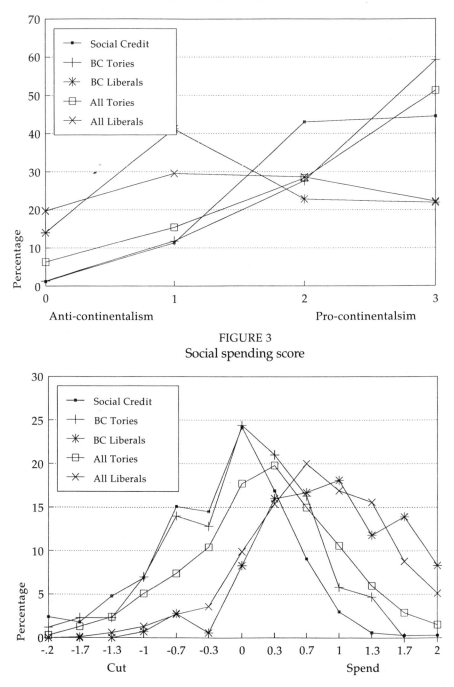

FIGURE 2
Continentalism scale score

FIGURE 3
Social spending score

The scores in Figure 3 were calculated by assigning a score to each respondent depending on whether he or she favoured substantial increases (+2), slight increases (+1), the status quo (0), slight decreases (–1), or substantial decreases (–2) in spending on education, welfare, and daycare. Respondents' numbers for each question were then summed and divided by three in order to create a combined score in the original range (of –2 to +2). A high score indicates greater support for increased spending and more resistance to cuts. The average scores on the resulting index were –0.2 for Social Credit delegates, 0.0 for Conservative delegates from BC, +0.2 for all Conservative delegates, +0.8 for Liberal delegates as a group and +0.9 for Liberal delegates from BC.

The pattern suggested by these scores is different from the distributions on the continentalist scale illustrated in Figure 2 only in the slight shift of the Social Credit activists to the right of the BC Conservatives and the increased distance between these two groups and the national Conservative delegates. The national and BC Liberals remain very similar. A majority (over 80%) of the Liberals, regardless of level, favour increased spending compared to 55 per cent for Conservatives as a whole and under 40 per cent for BC Conservatives and Socreds.

CONCLUSION

The Social Credit party rests upon a group of political activists who lean to a definite centre-right position on the political spectrum, exhibit homogeneity on some major issues, but are divided on a number of substantive questions including items related to government restraint and deregulation. They are also people with clear ideological links with Conservative activists in federal politics. The strength of the left may have helped drive federal and provincial party systems apart in British Columbia, but they have apparently not severed the ideological connections between the parties of the right.

The parties which have dominated recent federal and BC provincial elections have attracted activists with remarkably similar views. While Social Crediters are, on average, located to the right of federal Conservative activists, in fact they share that position with Tory activists from their own province. Here is some evidence of a division in activists' attitudes associated with the federal character of Canadian political life, at least for the Conservatives. But given the pronounced similarity in views between Tories and Social Crediters in British Columbia, this effect seems to be primarily a function of regional divisions rather than jurisdictional ones. This conclusion, on the salience of regional as opposed to jurisdictional divisions, is supported by the evidence which suggests the various groups' internal differences of opinion are structured by a similar left/right ideological dimension.

Given the Social Credit party's electoral dependence on substantial numbers of federal Liberal voters, and the important contribution made by Liberals to the Social Credit revival following the NDP victory in 1972, the paucity of Liberals in the ranks of activists comes as a surprise. There are some, and they are clearly closer to the province's ideological center, but they are not numerous enough to affect the basic balance of opinion among the party's activists.

At least two factors may be responsible for this. Most Liberals may simply not feel welcome in a party whose leaders were prominent and persistent critics of federal Liberal policies during Pierre Trudeau's long period in office. Secondly, movement from the Liberal party to Social Credit during the 1970s realignment appears to have been primarily an elite phenomenon. The NDP may have even benefited more than Social Credit from the last stages of the collapse of the party's provincial support, reducing the pool of potential Social Credit party recruits.

This brings us back to one of our fundamental questions. Is Social Credit really BC's provincial Conservative party rather than a genuine coalition? At the level of activist ideology this analysis argues yes. Yet, perhaps surprisingly, party activists do not want to think it is. Or at least they do not believe that explicit recognition of the link would be to the advantage of the Social Credit party. Fewer than 7 per cent of our respondents favoured an association with the federal Conservative party. Perhaps activists recognize that while they are Conservative in attitudes and Conservative in federal party support, much of the party's electorate is not. Implicitly they seem to remember that during the days of formal coalition (1941–52) the Liberals were actually the senior partner. Maintaining the right's electoral coalition requires respecting the reality of that heritage. Without Liberal support, the gap between Social Credit and the NDP would surely shrink, greatly increasing the probability of an NDP victory.

While Social Credit activists are, at some level, aware of this dilemma, the implications of their ideological ties to the Conservatives would seem to pose potential problems for the party. They are more likely (other things being equal) to be attracted to leadership candidates who share their ideological conservatism but it is these candidates who may move the party away from positions with which the party's Liberal voters could feel comfortable. William

Vander Zalm represents some of these contradictions in the party. He was chosen, in part, by a party wanting to repudiate Bill Bennett's style of politics. Yet he too seemed determined to reassert Social Credit's conservative faith and retest the limits and patience of its Liberal wing. Halfway though his first term as premier, that part of the electoral coalition began to pass judgement. His conservatism led to six successive by-election defeats, some in long-time party strongholds, including Vancouver city districts that had long been represented by the Liberals Bill Bennett had enticed into Social Credit. It is these elites, preoccupied with the tasks of coalition-building, that pose the greatest threat to such ideological leadership.

CHAPTER FIVE

The New Democrats: What Kind of Left?

As the left-wing alternative in a province with a tradition of radical socialist activity, British Columbia's New Democratic Party presents a set of conflicting images. On the one hand the party projects a middle-of-the-road image. This is suggested by the party's strength in the electorate, its considerable appeal to voters whose attachments at the national level remain with the Liberal party, and actions such as its support in the British Columbia legislature for the entrenchment of property rights in the Canadian constitution. On the other hand, a more radical image is suggested by its historical roots and is reinforced by events such as the endorsement, in the early 1970s, of the Waffle manifesto by the provincial party leader, Dave Barrett, or the 1975 national leadership convention in which BC's Rosemary Brown was clearly the left-wing alternative to Ed Broadbent, the choice of the national establishment.

The BC party has also been variously characterized in terms of its internal politics. Pictured as a homogeneous group compared to the kind of coalition the Social Credit party represents, the NDP is said to embody less of the diversity of opinion among the British Columbia electorate than does its opponents. But it is also seen as a party often split by the kinds of ideological and organizational divisions that plague left-wing parties, especially those not in power. These include divisions between traditional left and right wings of the party; between those committed to trade union issues and strong links between the party and organized labour, and those whose trade union sympathies are weak; differences based on what might be called new-left or life-style issues; and, more recently, divisions between environmentalists and those concerned with job preservation.

To what extent the party, and in particular the party activists, conforms to these various images is the subject of this chapter. Does opinion in the BC NDP differ from that in the national party? Is there diversity of opinion within this provincial party and what, if any, social basis is evident for such diversity? We explore the ideology of our NDP delegates first in comparison to their counterparts at the national level and then with respect to each other. The data for our national comparisons come from a survey of delegates to the NDP biennial convention held a month earlier in Montreal.[1]

PROVINCIAL NEW DEMOCRATS AND THEIR FEDERAL PARTY

Unlike its principal opponent in provincial politics, the NDP faces none of the potential conflict posed by provincial party activists who belong to competing national parties. Thus while the Social Credit party may house both federal Conservatives and federal Liberals (to say nothing of a smattering from right-wing federal fringe parties), the NDP constitution specifically provides that its members belong to no other political party. In practice, this tends to mean there is considerable overlap in the membership that is active in the party at the provincial level and those who are active at the federal level. This is certainly illustrated in our survey of the BC convention: over 80 per cent of the delegates indicated they had worked for the party in a federal campaign, and 34 per cent of them had, at some time, attended a federal party convention.

The fact that the same set of activists constitute the party organization in both provincial and federal politics raises its own interesting problems for the party. The NDP does not attract the same electorate at both levels (Blake 1985): it is typically some 25 per cent larger in provincial contests. Which of these electorates the organization best represents is not clear. This is important to the NDP for it, unlike the Socreds or the old-line national parties, has its decision-making structures shaped by membership numbers and the principles of representativeness.

The BC New Democrats who attend national party conventions must feel very much at home, for in many respects national party delegates resemble those who attend provincial gatherings. The delegates to both conventions from which we have data tended to be middle-aged, male, and better educated than the electorate. The survey of national delegates included more young (under thirty) delegates than did the provincial survey, 18 per cent compared to 9, but more than half the respondents to both questionnaires were over forty. In both samples two-thirds of the respondents were men, and 46 and 48 per cent, respectively, of the provincial and federal activists had one or more university degrees.

As would be expected in an organization which prizes commitment and service, convention delegates at both levels were long-time party members. Almost two-thirds of each group had been party members for eight or more years, and about one-third had been members for over fifteen years. The phenomenon of union affiliation in the NDP, which typically gives NDP conventions a unionist cast, was also evident in both delegate groups, albeit union members constituted a larger proportion of national delegates compared to provincial ones (45–36%).

Similarities between the two groups of New Democrats do not end with their social characteristics. They extend to their ideological profiles as well. Although limited by the number of similar questions in the two surveys, our comparisons of opinion among national and provincial convention delegates show few differences. What differences exist appear to be a function of the different contexts of a national and a provincial party rather than any fundamental ideological differences between British Columbia and Canadian New Democrats.

Eight indicators, tapping issues in the areas of social welfare, unemployment, education, and relations with the U.S. provide for comparison between the provincial and national delegates. The evidence (Table 14) shows opinion among both sets of activists was in favour of the expansion of social programs, against social security based on need, and was nationalist as opposed to continentalist on questions of Canadian independence and free trade. Differences are evident only in the strength (but not direction) of opinion and/or the proportions of undecided respondents in each group and the difference index scores are extraordinarily low.

Slightly more ambivalence was evident among the national delegates compared to those in BC on freer trade with the U.S. and whether or not the unemployed could find a job if they really wanted to, however the general thrust on both these issues was still a substantial level of consensus against free trade and against blaming the unemployed for their joblessness. The questions on which it could be argued some real differences do appear are those concerned with education spending and welfare rates, but these are questions where the political context may have played some role. In both questionnaires, the delegates were asked to indicate whether government spending in these areas should be increased, maintained, or decreased, but no specific government or governments were mentioned. It is likely that the primary point of reference for

TABLE 14

Distribution of attitudes among provincial New Democrats,
federal New Democrats, and federal New Democrats from BC

	Provincial NDP	All federal NDP	Difference scores	BC federal NDP
Adequate housing for everyone				
agree	95%	97%		98%
disagree	3	1		1
no opinion	2	2	.02	1
Unemployed could find jobs				
agree	2	8		5
disagree	97	82		88
no opinion	1	10	.15	7
Need-based social security				
agree	30	23		21
disagree	65	70		74
no opinion	4	6	.07	5
Expand childcare substantially	67	93	.13	94
Preserve independence even at cost of cut in living standard				
agree	83	77		78
disagree	9	11		11
no opinion	9	12	.06	11
Should have freer trade with U.S.				
agree	12.	14		15
disagree	81	68		61
no opinion	7	18	.13	23
Education spending				
increase substantially	78	46		54
increase somewhat	20	45		43
spend the same	2	8		3
decrease	0	1	.32	0
Welfare rates				
increase substantially	68	42		45
increase somewhat	29	45		44
stay the same	2	12		5
decrease	0	1	.27	0

NOTE: The difference scores compare provincial New Democrats with all federal New
Democrats. Larger difference scores indicate a greater difference between groups.

most delegates to the BC convention was spending by the British Columbia government. Among delegates to the national convention, the governments of reference were likely more variable, including both federal and provincial.

That the reference points were different for activists at the national convention is suggested by the pattern of responses among British Columbia delegates to that convention. Their pattern is very similar to that of the national group as a whole with only a slight tendency for their responses to lean more in the direction of opinion among the delegates at the BC convention. Clearly, these comparisons of provincial and national activists provide little support for contentions that BC New Democrats are outside the mainstream of the national party.

IDEOLOGICAL COHESION AMONG BC NEW DEMOCRATS

The ideological profile of the NDP activists that emerges above is one which suggests not only cross-level similarities between wings of the party but also considerable internal solidarity within the provincial party. The levels of support for social programs and nationalist sentiments are high, suggesting little dissent on issues that are the mainstay of social democratic rhetoric in Canada.

A look at responses to a larger array of such questions posed to our provincial sample does nothing to diminish this portrait of a party highly agreed in its support for welfare issues, programs for disadvantaged groups, and concern to protect Canadian independence and limit continentalist ties (see Table 15). Using the index of consensus developed for the analysis of Social Credit, we find only two questions on which there was any substantive difference of opinion within the BC New Democrats. First, with respect to need-based social security, a substantial minority (30%) agreed that social security programs such as old age pensions and family allowance should be based on need rather than the principle of universality, while 65 per cent were opposed to such an idea. On the other question, maintaining the size of government in BC, 35 per cent disagreed with the 52 per cent who were willing to see tax increases to maintain the current size.

Delegate opinion on spending levels in various areas of government activity reflected the general pattern of consensus described above. Large majorities favoured increased spending on social programs, on job creation grants, and on reforestation programs, but this consensus broke down over spending on tourism and highways: areas closely linked with Social Credit spending priorities. Here 48

TABLE 15
Policy consensus among NDP activists

	Per cent agree	Consensus index
Don't spend tax dollars on the sick	0.5	49.5
Unemployed could find jobs if they really wanted to	2.2	47.8
Government should guarantee standard of living	96.8	46.8
Government should see everyone has adequate housing	95.4	45.4
Many welfare programs are unnecessary	4.8	45.2
Foreign ownership threatens independence	95.4	45.4
Government should help women	92.0	42.0
Government should help jobless find work	90.5	40.5
Should have freer trade with U.S.	11.5	38.5
Favour law to balance budget	16.1	33.9
Preserve independence Canada even at cost of cut in standard of living	82.6	32.6
Free trade agreement with U.S. would restrict workers' rights	82.0	32.0
The community should support seniors	81.6	31.6
People should rely on selves not government	20.2	29.8
Social security should be based on need	30.2	19.8
Size of BC government should be kept even if means tax increase	52.0	2.0

NOTE: The consensus index can range from 50 (completely united) to 0 (completely split). For exact question wording see the Appendix.

and 49 per cent respectively supported retention of existing spending levels while the rest of our delegates were split between those favouring decreases and those supporting increases in these areas (see Table 20 for a comparative analysis).

New Democratic opinion on the regulatory activities of government appears to be less homogeneous. There was widespread support for greater regulation in the areas of the environment, human rights, and land use, but there was less agreement on controls over the marketing of agricultural produce and on regulation in lifestyle areas (gambling, shopping hours, and sale of alcohol). (See Table 19 for the detailed breakdown on these issues.)

Given the potential for differences in the party over environmental issues, the results on this question are perhaps surprising. But the considerable support (82%) for 'substantial extension' in regulation directed towards environmental protection was echoed in another environmental question we put to the delegates. When asked to choose between the statements: 'people who constantly argue for a clean environment just don't understand this means less investment and fewer jobs' or 'if having cleaner air means less money for me then that's the way it has to be,' 93 per cent of our respondents chose the environmentalist response. Although our questions may be too hypothetical to tap the kinds of divisions that could develop in the event of a more specific issue in which there are clear trade-offs between jobs and the environment, they do provide prima facie evidence that party activists will not be happy with a leadership that opts for jobs on such an issue.

Whereas responses concerning the environment elicit little evidence of internal division those concerned with agricultural marketing are more mixed. The figures here are interesting given the dilemma such marketing regulation might seem to pose for the party. Marketing boards, which regulate the sale of agricultural produce, apparently pit the interests of urban consumers, for whom they represent higher food prices, against those of producer groups, for whom they mean income stability. As a party, the NDP straddles both those interests. Its national roots involved an alliance of farmers' groups with labour as well as ideological commitments to economic planning. Yet it is now a party whose electoral base is primarily urban consumers. Reflecting this, our delegates were clearly less enthusiastic about the extension of such marketing regulation than they were about extending environmental regulation or expanding land use limitations. Only 57 per cent favoured the extension of government regulation over the marketing of agricultural products, compared to 90 per cent favouring more land use regulation and more than 95 per cent favouring more environmental regulation. Of the delegates who did not support expanding agricultural regulation, most (70%) favoured the status quo. There is some suggestion here of a rural/urban difference, but the correlations between our measures were weak,[2] and certainly the diversity of opinion on this issue was considerably less in the NDP than it was in the Social Credit sample. Among that group the modal opinion (36%) to reduce 'substantially' marketing regulation is matched by the 34 per cent who want at least some extension of such regulation.

Like the question on agricultural marketing, the responses of the NDP delegates to questions concerning regulation in lifestyle areas suggest some diversity of opinion, but the pattern of this diversity is mixed. For example, there was majority support (56%) for the status quo with respect to liquor sales, with more delegates in support of extending than reducing regulation (26% compared to 18%). Support for the status quo on shopping hours was somewhat lower (48%) and divisions between those favouring more rather than less regulation (24% compared to 28%) were sharper. Opinion on the regulation of gambling was even more divided: only 25 per cent preferred the status quo, 44 per cent supported extending such regulation and 32 per cent wanted it reduced.

These three regulatory items in lifestyle areas can be seen as involving different analytical dimensions: for example, the item on shopping hours raises the issue of employees' working conditions, gambling regulation the tendency of gambling to exploit the poor, and alcohol sales the relationship between unfettered distribution and alcohol abuse. But they can also be interpreted as questions whose main theme is a new-left dimension – which pits traditionalists against those who value the social freedoms at issue. To test the proposition that these items tap a new-left dimension, all our regulatory items together with three populism items were subjected to factor analysis. The analysis suggested that these lifestyle items form a distinct dimension, separate from all the other questions[3]. This indicates to us that, unlike the Socreds, among New Democrats opinion about government regulation is not driven by a single underlying disposition and, further, that some differences within the party can be characterized in terms of a lifestyle/social freedom dimension.

Turning to unions, we found New Democrats again highly agreed on a number of issues, but still divided over a few. There was virtual unanimity in the view that management should not be allowed to hire workers to take the place of strikers during a strike and that trade unions do not have too much power in British Columbia. Most (87%) of these New Democrats also believed that we need big unions because big corporations have so much power. However, 73 per cent did agree that unions should be required to have a secret ballot before taking strike action, a position that is sometimes rejected by union leaders.

On questions concerning the right to strike among public sector workers our delegates were more divided. As is apparent from Table 16, there were few New Democrats who would completely withhold the right to strike for any of the groups we identified and there was considerable agreement that government employees, teachers, and ferry workers should have an unrestricted right to strike. The latter are particularly significant in British Columbia because of the central role played by the government-owned ferry system in linking dozens of coastal and island communities as well as Vancouver

Island and the mainland. Differences arose over the rights of hospital workers and nurses, and, although less pronounced, with respect to police and firefighters.

TABLE 16
NDP activist opinion on restrictions on the right to strike
(horizontal percentages)

Group	Unrestricted	Some restrictions	No right to strike
Police	32	63	4
Firefighters	34	61	5
Nurses	42	56	2
Hospital workers	50	49	1
Ferry workers	71	28	1
Teachers	72	28	1
Government employees	80	20	1

The question of party relations with organized labour also elicited mixed replies. We asked our respondents whether they considered the party's ties to the labour movement were a factor in its failure to win the 1986 election. Forty-four per cent said the ties were very important or somewhat important in this failure. This group were more likely than the remaining delegates to agree that unions should be required to have secret ballots before strikes and that unions have too much power. They were also more likely to disagree with the claim that big unions are necessary. But these relationships are weak and the latter two are not statistically significant. This is not surprising given the few New Democrats who disagree with the pro-union view on these items. It seems then that while mainstream New Democrats show few anti-union sentiments, a large minority of even apparently pro-labour delegates make a connection between the party's failure at the polls and its ties with organized labour.[4]

To tap dimensions of more traditional left-wing/right-wing differences in the party we asked a number of questions on government ownership and private property. The pattern of responses among the delegates again suggests some agreement, but a number of points of disagreement. Most New Democrats (76%) concurred with the proposition that one of the main reasons for poverty is that the economy is based on private ownership and profits, but they differed in the extent of public ownership they would support. For example, we asked them whether a number of government-owned corporations should remain under government ownership, should be in private hands, or be run by some combination of the two. There was considerable agreement on keeping liquor stores and BC Rail (which has been publicly-owned for most of this century) under complete public ownership, but over 40 per cent of the respondents thought some or all of two government corporations – BC Place (Vancouver's covered sports stadium) and Whistler Corporation (which owns the convention centre in Whistler, BC, a major ski resort) – should be privately owned. There was even more diversity of opinion with respect to extending public ownership over a number of what are now privately owned companies. Only one company, BC Telephone, was targeted for complete public ownership by a majority (73 per cent) of the delegates. For the other three companies, respondents were quite mixed in their views of the preferred ownership pattern.

Our final group of items, those exploring populism in the party, turned out to be among the most contentious for these New Democrats. We have already argued that NDP traditions, as found in the CCF, are ambivalent on populism issues. Democratic commitments to grassroots control within the party were combined with the need for technical and bureaucratic experts to administer the programs of the welfare state. In addition, as we have seen in Chapter 3 (Table 3), a growing proportion of NDP activists are from the cadre of well-educated professionals who administer the modern state.

On none of our populism items did we find the level of consensus typical of most other questions. Fifty-two per cent of the delegates said they did not 'trust the simple, down-to-earth thinking of ordinary people rather than the theories of experts and intellectuals,' but 32 per cent said they did; 48 per cent did not think that we need 'a government that gets the job done without all this red tape,' but 37 per cent did. However, a plurality, 48 per cent, thought that bringing government back to the grassroots could solve most of our problems compared to 36 per cent who did not. Though distrust of experts and bureaucratic structures was minority opinion while predilection for grassroots problem-solving was a majority sentiment, factor analysis of these items with a number of others suggests the three populist questions do share a common dimension as they did in the case of Social Credit.

EXPLORING DIVERSITY IN THE NDP

Although BC New Democrats do demonstrate considerable internal homogeneity across a wide range of political issues, we have identified some areas of opinion where differences exist. To explore these areas further, we created attitude scales using those items on which differences of opinion were most apparent, and on which factor analysis indicated item commonality (see the Appendix for details of scale construction). These scales are listed (Table 17) in order of decreasing consensus and include: *public ownership*, using the public ownership questions on each of the private companies we listed and two of the public companies; *lifestyle regulation*, based on the items described earlier; *strike restriction*, using the right-to-strike questions on the police, nurses, hospital workers, and firefighters; *populism*, using the items discussed above; and *downsize*, created from the questions on need-based social security programs and on maintaining the size of government.

While New Democrats are generally agreed on many items central to a social democratic agenda, including extensive social programs and a large state sector, this last dimension provides evidence of a growing concern for the level of taxes and expenditures. Although this concern, at least as registered in these items, is still minority opinion it may be the most divisive issue within the party. The coefficient of variation is higher for this scale than any, including the populism one. To the extent Social Credit is able to make these issues salient in the wider electorate, they may be able to exploit NDP ambivalence.

TABLE 17

Attitudinal divisions among NDP activists by issue domain

Scale	Mean	Standard deviation	Coefficient of variation	N
Public ownership	7.23	3.44	.48	338
Lifestyle regulation	3.15	1.63	.52	360
Strike restriction	2.53	1.95	.77	369
Populism	1.34	1.09	.81	225
Downsize	.74	.73	.99	296

NOTE: See Appendix for details of scale construction.

Conflicting views about restrictions on the right to strike for various essential service workers is another especially divisive issue. This is a dimension with potentially larger ramifications for the party organization as there is modest evidence that this split follows a union/non-union division among party activists. The correlation coefficient between this scale and a union/non-union variable is 0.16

(sig.=.002). When the scale is dichotomized into high and low scores, 63 per cent of union members scored low (indicating reluctance to place restrictions with respect to strikes) compared to 47 per cent of non-union delegates.

In order to see if these various dimensions might provide the grounds for mutually reinforcing tensions within the party, correlation coefficients were computed for all pairs of the scales. The scale intercorrelations (Table 18) are weak, with the new-left index in particular unrelated to any other dimension we measured. There is, however, the hint of a left/right split in the relationships between views on public ownership, restrictions on public sector strikes and downsizing government. Those most favourable to public ownership were least supportive of restrictions with respect to strikes and least likely to show support for limiting the size of government. But there was no evidence for a consistent social basis – such as one related to occupation, union membership, or even generation – to these left/right ideological elements in the party. Nor was any regional element detected. Indeed, while there was a weak relationship between union membership and views on strike restrictions, with union members tending to indicate what may be considered left-wing views, there was also a (weak) relationship between union membership and scores on the downsize scale with union members *more* likely to score in a right-wing direction.

The only other social variable that showed any relationship to scores on these scales was gender. Women's scores on the public ownership scale were higher than those of men.[5]

TABLE 18
Correlations among attitude scales for NDP activists

Scale	Lifestyle regulation	Strike restriction	Populism	Downsize government
Public ownership	.07	–.20*	.05	–.20*
Lifestyle regulation		–.06	–.05	–.09
Strike restriction			–.10	.06
Populism				.22*

NOTE: Coefficients marked with an asterisk are significant at .05 level.

While the issues which divided these delegates were not generally related to region, class, or other social variables, they were related, not surprisingly, to the question of party strategy and what sort of direction the party should take. When we asked the delegates whether they agreed or disagreed with the statement that the party has to be careful not to move too far to the left, we found surprisingly little consensus. Forty-four per cent of our respondents agreed with the statement, but 50 per cent disagreed. Those with higher scores on the downsize and strike restriction scales were more likely to agree the party must be careful about moving left, while those who scored high on the public ownership and even the lifestyle regulation scales were less likely to agree with the statement. When issues of strategy arise in the party it appears that they reflect some of the NDP's internal ideological differences as well.

CONCLUSION

The BC New Democrats in our sample belie any reputation for ideological distinctiveness within the family of New Democrats nationally. Their responses to virtually all issue questions posed to both national and provincial delegates were distributed in very much the same manner as those of their national counterparts. Delegates from both groups indicated high levels of support for the social democratic agenda of an expansive welfare state combined with an antipathy to continentalism in its various forms. Within the BC New Democrats this image of a party highly agreed on social programs was extended to include agreement on spending priorities, a number of areas of government regulation and most union-related issues.

But while the New Democrats did display a considerable degree of consensus across a broad range of issues, some areas did remain divisive. Populism items, which arguably deal more with matters of style than substance, and regulation questions related to lifestyle issues elicited diverse responses among delegates. Disagreement exists with respect to labour issues such as restrictions on strikes in essential service areas as well as over the appropriate scope of public ownership in the province. But the most divisive questions, and perhaps the ones with the most potential for party conflict, were those which touched on restrictions and limits on government and social programs for fiscal reasons. Related to questions of party strategy, both implicitly in the content of the questions and explicitly in delegates' responses to our strategy question, issues which pose hard fiscal choices are ones which may bedevil future consensus in the party.

CHAPTER SIX

The Liberals:
Centre or Fringe?

ANTHONY M. SAYERS WITH THE AUTHORS

Liberals in British Columbia are placed in an awkward position. Ideologically ill-suited to participate in the polarized politics of the province, and unable to extract support from their party's federal electorate, they seem destined to play a bit part in provincial politics. It is within this context that the Liberal party of British Columbia struggles to exist.

We will suggest that the Liberals rely on an elite group of activists who occupy a version of the middle ground in British Columbia. Somewhat surprisingly given the migration of their legislative leaders to Social Credit in the 1970s, Liberal activists resemble the NDP more than Social Credit. As well, they embody some of the tensions between welfare and business liberalism associated with the Liberal party by Christian and Campbell (1983). While the structure of opinion within the party on economic questions is relatively heterogeneous, there is a tendency for Liberals to be united in adopting a federal or national perspective on other issues.

The Liberals' place in the middle of the polarized politics of British Columbia makes it difficult for them to capitalize on any ideological distinctiveness they might possess. In a party system organized in part to contain and frustrate a strong left, any third party is placed at a strategic disadvantage. Thus the Liberals have become victims of a context they helped to create. They were the dominant partner in the coalition era which produced polarization, but once they lost their privileged position as the major bulwark against the left they have been consigned to the fringes of the system.

LIBERAL ACTIVISTS AND POLARIZED POLITICS

The Liberal party currently receives about 5 per cent of the vote in provincial elections. That makes it virtually irrelevant in electoral politics, seen by most observers as a small centre party with little significance except as a place where some temporarily park their declared preferences between elections. The notion of a party being banished to the wilderness of the middle ground of the political spectrum is somewhat ironic. Successful Canadian national parties have traditionally sought to capture the middle ground to ensure electoral success. The strategic context in BC prevents that by making the centre essentially a marginal position.

The first task of this chapter is to demonstrate that the Liberals are indeed a centre party in provincial politics. This requires an assessment of the relative position of the party vis-à-vis the NDP and Social Credit parties. By implication this leads to an analysis of the nature of the middle ground in British Columbian politics.

The NDP and Social Credit in British Columbia represent parties whose provincial branches are the principal contenders for office but whose federal partners are not. The NDP can claim some national prominence given it takes 35 per cent of the BC vote in national elections, but Social Credit is now non-existent nationally. The Liberals face the reverse situation – they are a major party federally but a minor party provincially. Not only is the Liberal party distinct in this way, but its development separates it from the two major provincial parties.

The Liberal party is an insider party. During its early more successful period in British Columbia, it developed, as did its counterpart in federal politics, from coalition-building among elites within the legislature. The structure of the extra-parliamentary party became institutionalized only after elected politicians built their alliances. In contrast, the NDP and Social Credit are outsider parties. Their ancestors emerged from the extra-parliamentary mass movements of the 1920s and 1930s within Canada, and their development was shaped by the economic and social factors peculiar to those provinces and regions which gave them birth (Young 1978).

As demonstrated in Chapter 10, the exigencies of a two-party system driven by conflict between left and right, has encouraged the two main provincial parties to mimic each other in a number of ways. The fact remains, however, that they are also, to some degree, both populist parties. Hence any single dichotomy may not truly capture the essence of the distinction between them and the Liberal party. Three factors come under scrutiny here: the place of the Liberals on the left/right ideological spectrum; the ideological distance between the Liberals and the other two parties; and how the Liberals look from the perspective of populism.

A key element in conflict between left and right concerns the role of the state, including the degree of support for government regulation, and debate over the magnitude and objects of government expenditure. Table 19 details inter-party differences regarding regulation. It contains two sets of figures. One is the percentage of activists from each of the three provincial parties favouring different degrees of government regulation. The second is a measure of the opinion distance between Liberal activists and activists from each of the other provincial parties.

Two general observations can be made about this table. First, the Liberals do tend to fall between the NDP and Social Credit activists, and secondly, on average they appear to be closer to the NDP position. The average Liberal/NDP difference index is 0.23 compared to an average Liberal/Socred difference of 0.38.

Social Credit activists tend to support the status quo or a reduction in government regulation though overall they are quite divided with no cell on any question accounting for more than 58 per cent of the Social Credit activists. NDP activists present a different picture. As a group they tend to support higher levels of government regulation. On environmental protection, human rights and land use at least 90 per cent favour extended government regulation; on the other issues, the NDP activists either supported the status quo or favoured extended regulation. (See chapters 4 and 5 for detailed analysis of intra-party differences in the large parties.)

Liberal/NDP similarities (and Liberal/Social Credit differences) were clearest in the case of support for increased environmental protection with 97 per cent of NDP activists and 92 per cent of the Liberal activists taking this position compared to only a quarter of the Socreds. The Liberal/Social Credit difference index score on this issue (0.68) is the largest in the table. Extension of human rights regulations was supported by fewer Liberals than New Democrats, but their differences are less than half the Liberal/Social Credit difference. Barely 11 per cent of Social Credit activists favour increased protection of human rights. With the exception of attitudes towards marketing of agricultural products, the only areas where the Liberals are close to Social Credit (gambling, shopping hours, and sale of alcohol) are also areas where they are not all that different from New Democrats.

A further measure of the relative positions of the parties on regulation issues is provided by the anti-regulation scale. This combines the responses to all the regulation items and has a possible range from –2 (strongly favour strengthening regulation in all areas) to +2

TABLE 19

Attitudes towards government regulation by party
(horizontal percentages)

Policy area		Substantially extend	Slightly extend	Keep as now	Slightly reduce	Substantially reduce	DI
Environmental	NDP	82.4	14.3	3.0	.3	0.0	.26
protection	Liberal	56.3	35.6	4.6	2.3	1.1	
	Socred	7.2	16.5	44.9	21.0	10.5	.68
Land use	NDP	59.0	30.7	7.1	3.0	.3	.27
	Liberal	31.7	31.7	31.7	3.7	1.2	
	Socred	4.5	17.6	23.2	31.8	22.9	.50
Human rights	NDP	71.4	23.8	4.1	.5	.3	.33
protection	Liberal	37.9	37.9	20.7	1.1	2.3	
	Socred	2.1	8.7	52.8	20.6	15.8	.65
Sale of	NDP	10.7	15.3	56.3	11.7	6.0	.15
alcohol	Liberal	7.9	14.6	44.9	16.9	15.7	
	Socred	8.4	17.4	27.5	18.0	28.7	.17
Marketing of	NDP	28.7	28.1	32.0	9.3	2.0	.29
agricultural	Liberal	7.1	21.4	31.0	28.6	11.9	
products	Socred	21.1	12.4	8.8	22.1	35.6	.38
Shopping	NDP	8.5	15.6	47.5	18.9	9.4	.15
hours	Liberal	12.6	14.9	39.1	12.6	20.7	
	Socred	9.2	12.4	30.5	12.1	35.8	.15
Gambling	NDP	29.6	13.6	24.7	10.3	21.7	.18
	Liberal	11.2	18.0	34.8	13.5	22.5	
	Socred	17.8	22.0	24.3	16.0	19.9	.13

NOTE: The DI scores are difference indexes comparing Liberal activists with Social Credit and the NDP. The larger the difference score, the greater the difference between attitudes of activists in the two parties from the Liberals. For details on the index see Chapter 4.

Ns vary slightly given different amounts of missing data. However, percentages in the table are based approximately on 370 New Democrats, 335 Socreds, and 88 Liberals.

(strongly favour deregulation in all areas). The overall impression of the Liberals' central position on regulation is confirmed by an examination of a graphic representation of party activists' responses on this scale (Figure 4). Moreover, the Liberal distribution has a greater overlap with the NDP than with Social Credit.

FIGURE 4
Attitudes towards government regulation

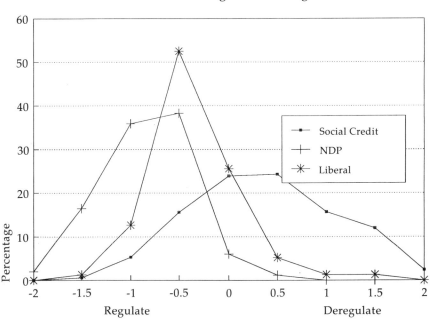

Table 20 presents the delegates perspectives on the issue of government spending. However, the pattern of responses is a little more complex than in the case of regulation. The percentages show the Liberals falling between the NDP and the Social Credit respondents but with no real difference in the average of the difference indexes – 0.34 for the Liberal/Socred comparison and 0.33 for the Liberal/NDP one. On education, a clear majority of Liberals and New Democrats favoured increased spending, whereas most Socreds favoured the status quo producing a Liberal/NDP difference score of 0.20 compared to 0.60 for the Liberal/Social Credit comparison. The same pattern (though smaller difference scores for both comparisons) characterizes attitudes towards daycare and health care spending. The results for the daycare question were almost identical for the NDP and Liberals activists (a majority favour increases), while a substantial number of Social Credit delegates actually favour spending cuts.

On welfare rates, the story is somewhat different. The distance between the Liberal and Social Credit activists over welfare rates is quite large (DI=0.50). While the Liberals may not seem particularly

TABLE 20
Attitudes towards government spending by party

Policy area		Substantially increase	Slightly increase	Keep as now	Slightly reduce	Substantially reduce	DI
Education	NDP	77.7	19.8	2.1	.3	0.0	.20
	Liberal	58.0	34.1	8.0	0.0	0.0	
	Socred	4.2	27.4	54.5	7.8	6.0	.60
Welfare	NDP	68.0	29.3	2.4	0.0	.3	.48
rates	Liberal	19.5	46.0	27.6	5.7	1.1	
	Socred	.9	14.3	48.2	21.1	15.5	.40
Health care	NDP	57.7	35.5	6.2	.5	0.0	.37
	Liberal	20.7	52.9	21.8	4.6	0.0	
	Socred	3.3	29.0	59.8	5.7	2.1	.41
Reforestation	NDP	86.2	12.4	1.4	0.0	0.0	.36
	Liberal	50.6	34.5	9.2	3.4	2.3	
	Socred	44.0	40.1	13.9	.9	1.2	.10
Job creation	NDP	58.5	24.0	11.5	3.0	3.0	.44
grants	Liberal	14.5	32.5	24.1	16.9	12.0	
	Socred	19.8	25.5	30.3	8.7	15.6	.15
Highways	NDP	7.0	21.1	49.2	16.2	6.5	.18
	Liberal	1.1	9.1	48.9	29.5	11.4	
	Socred	11.0	27.1	55.4	6.0	.6	.34
Tourism	NDP	6.3	22.3	48.4	14.7	8.4	.10
	Liberal	9.3	22.1	55.8	11.6	1.2	
	Socred	24.7	30.1	39.9	2.7	2.7	.25
Public	NDP	14.3	56.0	29.1	.3	.3	.49
service	Liberal	0.0	21.4	65.5	8.3	4.8	
salaries	Socred	1.2	13.6	54.3	17.2	13.6	.19
Daycare	NDP	66.7	28.0	5.1	0.0	.3	.39
	Liberal	27.9	44.2	25.6	1.2	1.2	
	Socred	3.6	14.0	46.1	13.4	22.9	.54

NOTE: See notes to Table 19.

close to the NDP position either (DI=0.48), a majority of Liberals and New Democrats favour increased spending, whereas a only a small proportion of Socreds do.

The Liberals are closer to the Social Crediters with regard to economic development issues like reforestation and job creation grants for business. In both cases New Democrats are much more willing to spend than Liberals or Socreds. However, a plurality of Liberals and Socreds support spending increases for job creation as well, as do majorities in both parties in the case of funds for reforestation.

Tourism, which in British Columbia is an important economic development issue, finds Liberal and NDP activists happier with the present level of spending, 48 per cent and 56 per cent, respectively, endorsing this position (DI=0.10). By contrast, this is an area where a majority (53%) of Social Credit activists want more spending so that the difference from the Liberals is 0.25. A plurality among each of the three groups of activists favours the status quo with respect to spending on highways, but the Liberals and New Democrats were more likely to favour reductions than the Socred activists.

Overall, attitudes towards government spending present a complex picture. In the social policy areas the Liberals are most like the NDP. On education, they are quite close; where welfare, daycare, and health spending are concerned, Liberal support declines compared to the NDP but the difference index scores confirm that the Liberals are on average closer to the NDP in all four areas. The results for economic development issues: reforestation, highways spending, job creation grants, and tourism are also mixed. The Liberals are closer to the New Democrats on highways spending, but closer to Social Credit on reforestation and job creation grants.

Nevertheless, when the spending items are combined into a 'government spending' scale, the centre position of the Liberals is clearly evident (Figure 5). There also appears to be slightly more overlap between Social Credit and the Liberals on spending than was true for the government regulation scale.

Another measure of differences with regard to the left/right dimension utilized the 'collective versus individual responsibility' scale (see Appendix). Unlike the regulation and spending scales, this one attempts to measure more general attitudes towards support for state versus individual responsibility for individual well-being. On this scale, while between the two other parties on average, the Liberal activists are closer to the Social Credit position. The NDP mean is 0.39, the Liberal mean is 2.65, and the Social Credit mean is 3.74. Figure 6 offers a graphic representation of the differences between activist groups as well as the distribution of views within them. It confirms that Liberal activists straddle the centre, but their distribution of opinion is much flatter, indicating lesser ideological coherence, than is the case for the other two parties.

The final scale which measures populism complicates the other-

FIGURE 5
Attitudes towards government spending

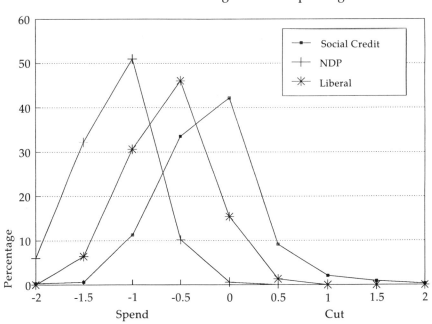

wise apparently straightforward polarization of BC politics. The means for the populism scale were 1.36, 1.5, and 2.34 for the NDP, Liberal, and Social Credit respectively. This suggests that Liberal delegates are relatively less populist than Social Credit and slightly more so than the NDP. However, it is clear from the distribution of activist opinion on this scale (Figure 7) that the story is at once more subtle and complex. It is Social Credit partisans who differ dramatically from the other two parties in their enthusiasm for populist positions. The Liberals, betraying their long history as the nation's government party, are the least populistic. The New Democrats on the whole are most ambivalent; their activists seem evenly spread out across a populist/non-populist continuum. Presumably it is this feature that has led the NDP to swing between leaders like Dave Barrett, ranked amongst the most populist actors of his generation, and Mike Harcourt who epitomizes professional, middle-class reasonableness.

Taken together, the evidence on all these dimensions clearly shows that Liberal activists do occupy the centre in British Columbia politics. Given their middle-class character, it may be surprising to some that they tend to favour the position of NDP activists on

FIGURE 6
Collective vs. individual responsibility

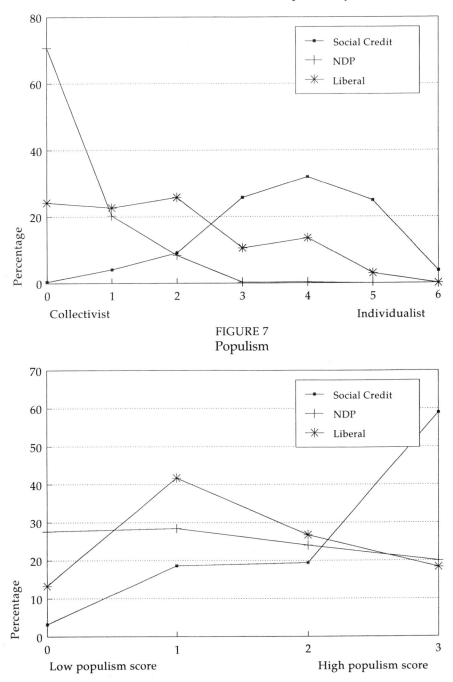

FIGURE 7
Populism

many of the issues looked at here. On questions of social policy, the Liberals are particularly inclined to approve of a pro-active role for government both with regards to spending and regulation. On other questions concerned with government regulatory activities, Liberals are more divided as a group, but on average they are closer to the NDP position. The issue of government spending linked to economic development issues like job creation grants and reforestation finds them closer to Social Credit.

COHESION AND DIVISION WITHIN THE PROVINCIAL LIBERAL PARTY

The first step in describing the structure of opinion within the party was to calculate a consensus index based on delegates' responses to a range of important policy and opinion questions. The first column gives the percentage agreeing with the given statement. The second column contains the CI scores which range from 46.6 (strong consensus) to 1.1 (sharp division).

The greatest divisions among Liberal delegates occurs over what might loosely be described as ideological issues. For example, the balance of power between unions and corporations has been a long-standing issue in British Columbia. And in response to a question asking whether big corporations require big unions to balance their power, Liberals were nearly evenly divided, with only 51.1 per cent agreeing that big corporations need to be offset by big unions. The Liberals were similarly divided on whether unions in British Columbia are too powerful, and over the right of management to hire replacement workers during strikes.

The Liberals' divisions on this issue distinguishes them from both NDP and Social Credit partisans who are united but on opposing sides of the issue. Moreover, it is significant that three of the nine issues on which the Liberals divide relate to this business/union tension that is a major driving force behind the polarization of the province's politics.

Liberals are also divided in their responses to welfare issues. Both the government provision of jobs for the unemployed as well as government support for seniors have low index scores, indicating a lack of internal party agreement. Social security based on need also splits Liberals evenly. This is consistent with the Liberals' ambiguous position as a group on whether individuals should rely on themselves or the government when they encounter difficulties in life. With regard to the problem of red tape in government, long a shibboleth of populist politics, Liberals are again evenly divided.

TABLE 21

Policy consensus among Liberal activists

	Per cent agree	Consensus index
Don't spend taxes on sick	3.4	46.6
Favour Canadian identity over regional identity	92.2	42.2
Favour Meech Lake Accord	7.8	42.2
Secret strike ballots for unions	92.2	42.2
Preserve independence even at cost of cut in standard of living	91.9	41.9
Favour BC position on Meech Lake	8.9	41.1
Favour free trade deal	8.9	41.1
Approve of official bilingualism	91.1	41.1
Poverty due to private ownership	12.2	37.8
Foreign ownership threatens independence	86.7	36.7
Clean environment regardless of costs	86.7	36.7
Negotiate native land claims	85.4	35.4
Favour BC decentralization	15.6	34.4
Many welfare programs unnecessary	19.5	30.5
Favour freer trade with U.S.	80.2	30.2
Favour BC privatization program	20.0	30.0
Support elected senate	80.0	30.0
Government regulation stifles initiative	21.4	28.6
Unemployed could find jobs if they really wanted to	21.8	28.2
Size of BC government should be kept even if means tax increase	22.2	27.8
Approve of public service bilingualism	75.6	25.6
Government should help women	75.3	25.3
Trust down-to-earth thinking	27.9	22.1
Government should guarantee standard of living	71.8	21.8
Favour law to balance budget	30.7	19.3
Public sector workers have more security	68.9	18.9
Maintain existing division of power	65.6	15.6
Government to provide housing	65.6	15.6
BC treated fairly by federal government	40.0	10.0
Rely on selves not government	59.8	9.8
Cut government red tape	59.3	9.3
Grassroots could solve problems	41.7	8.3
Social security should be based on need	56.7	6.7
Free trade will restrict workers' rights	46.7	3.3
Unions too powerful	47.1	2.9
Management should not hire workers during strike	47.8	2.2
Community should support seniors	48.8	1.2
Government should help jobless find work	51.1	1.1
Big corporations require big unions	51.1	1.1

NOTE: The consensus index can vary from 50 (completely united) to 0 (completely split). For exact question wording see the Appendix.

Strong support for the concept of private property and agreement with the demand that unions have secret strike ballots marks the existence of a free enterprise strand among the Liberal delegates. This is tempered by the Liberals' positive attitude towards welfare programs, which suggests support exists for welfare as a general principle. Liberal delegates were also united in supporting government time and money being spent on social policy matters such as environmental concerns and Native land claims.

Statements tapping attitudes to Canadian nationalism and independence, long the special appeal of the national party, evoked a much more cohesive response from Liberals. In fact, about half of the issues on which Liberals were substantially agreed deal with either these flag-type issues or matters that are probably of more concern for federal than for provincial politics. One of the most unifying issues for Liberals is the importance of Canadian as opposed to regional identity. Liberal activists are especially united in their support of pro-Canadian positions on questions concerning Canadian independence. This may reflect a combination of their anti-provincialist sentiment as well as disagreement with the particular policy preferences of the Social Credit government.

The first ministers' agreement to amend the constitution by recognizing Quebec as a distinct society (the Meech Lake Accord) had few Liberal supporters in BC during 1987 (7.8%), a homogeneous response repeated in the Liberals' disagreement with the provincial government's support of the Accord. 'Canadian independence at any cost' attracted strong support. The 'threat of foreign ownership' appears to have tripped the same reflex in Liberals, with 86.7 per cent agreeing that foreign ownership is a threat to Canadian independence.

Disagreement with the free trade deal negotiated by the national Conservative government is also quite strong and cohesive. However, this response seems to have been a reaction to the specific agreement negotiated with the United States and not an expression of opposition to free trade in principle, since there is considerable support for 'freer trade with the United States.' Two institutional issues generate widespread Liberal support: official bilingualism and an elected Senate.

The issues which most divide the Liberal delegates can be grouped under two headings. First, those which tend to structure attitudes and policy choices along a left-right continuum, and in particular issues which juxtapose the place of business and unions in society. The second group of issues which clearly divide the Liberal delegates are those dealing with traditional forms of welfare and the role of government generally: job grants, old age assistance, and the need to cut government red tape.

There thus appears to be a healthy strand of business liberalism within the provincial party. Despite the Liberals' disunity over some questions that present differing views of the power of business and unions, they were united in being favourably disposed towards the value of private property and suspicious of unions when the balance of power between management and unions is not at issue. Although united in their opposition to the national Conservative government's Free Trade Agreement, they still wanted freer trade with the United States.

A welfare liberalism element also exists in the provincial party. Although the Liberal delegates are divided on specific welfare issues, they are united in supporting the general idea of welfare programs. The division over specific welfare programs stands in contrast to the Liberals' united support of other social policy initiatives such as medicare, education spending, and publicly supported daycare.

What are we to make of this pattern of internal division and cohesion? The tension between welfare and business liberalism certainly appears in other provinces and characterizes the national Liberal party as well (Christian and Campbell 1983; Blake 1988; Johnston 1988). However, there is a continuum between those issues which divide and those which unite Liberal activists in British Columbia which appears somewhat unusual. At one end are questions that look something like left versus right questions – these evoke division. At the other extreme are issues relating to Canadian nationalism. However, the apparent cohesion on conceptions of the national community may simply be a function of the place of BC Liberals on issues such as Meech Lake and the free trade deal which are rather more divisive in the national party as a whole.

CONCLUSION

The heterogeneity amongst the Liberal activists on left/right issues is distinctive. This suggests that in the context of polarized provincial politics, there exists a group of activists whose opinions fit between the two major parties but overlap them as well. While, on average, the Liberal activists proved to be closer to the NDP than the Social Credit party especially regarding opinions of government regulation and social policy, there is a degree of fiscal conservatism and support for free enterprise which distinguishes the Liberals from the NDP activists and places them closer to the Socreds. Liberals are relatively more coherent on issues affecting definitions of the national political community such as bilingualism policy and the Meech Lake Accord. In this they resemble many British Columbian voters who manage to set aside left/right ideological differences in choosing sides in federal politics. This must be part of the reason their national vote share is four or five times greater than that in provincial elections.

Liberal closeness to the NDP is noteworthy given their own perception that they are competing for the Social Credit vote in the province. Their ideologically centrist and pro-federal characteristics highlight the difficulty of a party of the middle with a strong federal counterpart succeeding in a province where polarized politics is the norm; a norm which separates the provincial party system from the federal party system to which the Liberal party is much better suited. The Liberal party is neither ideologically suited nor strategically placed to deal with this type of political environment.

CHAPTER SEVEN

Leadership Selection in the BC Parties

The picture of BC politics we have drawn to this point is one of electoral politics pervaded by the rhetoric (and sometimes the substance) of polarization. It is also one of party activists who reflect and sustain the image of parties divided on many issues. The governing right-wing Social Credit party portrays itself as defending free enterprise against the socialist threat of the New Democrats, while the NDP opposition sees itself as offering a systematic alternative to the excesses of the business class. The Liberals, who have been virtually squeezed out of existence in this political climate, have sought to preserve a moderate centrist position. The province has a deeply ingrained populist streak in its political culture and such orientations profoundly affect the way its parties organize and operate (Blake 1985; Young 1983).

Perhaps as a consequence of their party being in power most of the time since 1952, Social Credit activists are a more heterogeneous lot than the NDP. Within the governing party there is support for a variety of positions and considerable divergence on matters of substance (especially social spending) and matters of political tactics. As we will find in Chapter 10, on most issues Social Credit reflects something of the variety of opinion found in the electorate, albeit a somewhat right-wing variant of it. New Democratic activists, on the other hand, share a set of opinions that are at once more homogeneous and more divergent from those held by the province's voters. In this sense the party might be said to be both more ideological and less responsive to the pressures of the electoral marketplace.

In such a system, party leaders must negotiate a particularly delicate tightrope. Partisans expect their vision of the public agenda to be forcefully articulated and the enemy ravaged by their champion, but electoral calculation might suggest a prudent moderation and an appeal to the more fainthearted. In both parties, leaders face a considerable majority (65% of Socreds, 74% of NDPers) who believe there is too great an emphasis on polls in politics, and substantial numbers who see no danger in moving their party further from the centre.

But as in other Canadian party systems, electoral competition in British Columbia focuses much on the personalities and character of the party leaders. And party members know it. When asked to indicate the importance of a series of factors in determining their choice for leader, delegates at the 1986 Social Credit leadership convention chose 'ability to win the next election' more often than any other factor; personal characteristics of the candidates were second. New Democrats, indicating why they thought they lost the 1986 election most often attributed it to the appeal of Social Credit leader Vander Zalm, and proclaimed the most important issue facing their party was improved public relations. In both instances policy considerations were relegated to a position of lesser importance.

It is not clear how party leader/follower relationships will be structured in such a system, or what the nature and basis of leadership conflict and selection will be. At least two, apparently contrary, possibilities suggest themselves. First, the highly ideological cast to British Columbia's politics might lead us to expect an equally ideological, issue-driven character to internal party organization and life. Given the centrality of leaders in shaping party direction this might be most clearly revealed in competitive struggles for the leadership. Leadership candidates would be chosen to the extent that they personified policy positions.

The alternative is a relatively issueless leadership politics. It may very well be that most of the ideological space in the system is found between the parties rather than within them. That being so, leadership candidates might be agreed on basic policy orientations and determined not to expose any possible internal fissures to their opponents. In such a case, the party would work to ensure that its leadership would not be highly contested; when it was, the divisions would revolve about organizational rather than ideological concerns. The uncontested NDP leadership succession in 1987 might be seen as an example of this type of selection process.

Of course British Columbia's parties may, at different times and in different situations, experience both types of leadership selection contests. Whatever the experiences of 1986 and 1987, one might expect that Social Credit would normally, as a pragmatic governing party, have rather non-ideological leadership contests. The New

Democrats, on the other hand, might be expected to have leadership contests marked by rather more ideological fervour.

For the Liberal party, struggling as it is to survive, the process of leadership selection raises quite different problems. Since the provincial leader has no realistic expectations of office, and in recent years not even a seat in the legislature, the problem for the party is to find and keep an able and credible leader. In Chapter 9, we demonstrate that the party is marked by divisions between those oriented to federal and provincial politics, and between what we call 'optimists' and 'realists' (see also So 1988). Both these dividing lines might well provide the basis for leadership conflict in the party. Certainly such splits contributed to the downfall of the provincial Conservatives in the 1940s and 1950s (Black 1979b).

In this chapter we look at the most recent cases of leadership change in British Columbia's three parties. This cross-party comparison allows us to determine which of the various scenarios is the better fit for Social Credit and the New Democrats and what, if any, dividing lines provide the basis for leadership conflict in the Liberal party. In the next chapter we offer a detailed examination of the internal dynamics of competition within the governing Social Credit party, the only one of the three to have had an open contest for the party leadership. But before exploring the internal leadership politics of the parties it is necessary to consider the convention process within which it occurs and the context of the leadership contests themselves.

LEADERSHIP CONVENTIONS AND THE POLITICAL CLASS IN BC

National party conventions have now been subject to considerable analysis (Perlin 1988) and those studies colour our understanding of the party leadership selection process generally. On the face of it, there are similarities between these national conventions and their provincial counterparts. In terms of a socio-economic profile, for example, the delegates at the BC leadership conventions seemed not significantly different from those who populate national conventions.

But this is a rather superficial resemblance. It disguises the fact that provincial party leadership conventions in BC, and we believe in other provinces, differ in other important ways from those held by the national parties (Carty, Erickson, and Blake 1991). It is important to identify these variations and how they affect the organization, the dynamics, and the outcomes of provincial contests. Compared to national party leadership conventions, those held in British Columbia are smaller, more simply structured, and dominated by experienced long-serving partisans. Any one of these features would distinguish their leadership campaigns and convention practices from those of the federal parties. Taken together, they produce a very different institution and process.

While national conventions, with thousands of delegates and alternates, have become so large as to be impersonal and in many ways unmanageable, the same is not true at the provincial level. The Social Credit convention with 1300 delegates was the largest of the three in BC, the Liberals with just over 200 was obviously just a family-sized affair. The New Democratic 1987 convention had about 750 delegates, roughly 30 per cent fewer than the Skelly convention in 1984, and well below the total number of delegates who were entitled to attend. The difference no doubt reflects the fact that the leadership was keenly contested in 1984 while Harcourt was acclaimed in 1987. These smaller conventions are inevitably more intimate events: delegates have more opportunity to talk to one another and to follow closely what is taking place on the floor of the convention.

Although we have only sketchy data on this, it seems likely that the smaller scale of these conventions must affect the campaigns that the candidates run. This is surely reinforced by the more restricted geographical space covered by provincial (as compared to national) parties. Certainly in Social Credit these factors appear to have engendered very close ties between delegates and candidates. Almost 60 per cent of the respondents in that party reported that they were 'actively involved in the leadership campaign of one of the candidates,' and 55 per cent said they had made a commitment 'to the candidate personally' for first ballot support. That degree and sense of personal involvement is not so possible in nation-wide leadership campaigns that are so professionally and bureaucratically managed.

In each of these provincial conventions, the social space was also considerably reduced by the number of delegates who were related to other delegates. In all three parties, the proportion of such delegates was at least 25 per cent, the majority being married couples. Surely most of these delegates do not behave and vote as autonomously as other delegates and their presence must considerably alter the social anthropology of the candidates' campaigns and the conventions. A hint of this can be seen in our Liberal data: delegates with relatives at the convention were significantly more satisfied with Wilson's leadership than were the others.[1] This is especially notable as it is one of the few dividing lines between delegates at that convention. We think this anthropological dimension of provincial leadership campaigns and conventions deserves further attention in future studies.

As well as being considerably smaller than recent national leadership selection conventions, those held by the BC parties have a much simpler internal structure. Not only are there far fewer ex-officio delegates but the categories of delegates are strictly limited (Table 22). There has not been the proliferation of interests with their special representation that has marked the national Liberal and Conservative parties which now have about twenty delegate categories (Courtney 1986). This makes the provincial party conventions rather harder to penetrate and offers candidates limited opportunity to invent new party organizations in an attempt to take over the party.[2]

TABLE 22

Structure of delegate representation at BC leadership conventions (vertical percentages)

	Social Credit	NDP	Liberal
Constituency delegates	100.0*	87.7	83.0*
Party executives/officials		2.5	11.4
Affiliated members		7.5	
Others		1.4*	5.7

NOTE: Categories marked with an asterisk include MLAS. The Liberal constituency delegate category consists of 45.5% from provincial and 37.5% from federal constituency associations.

Whatever else this simplified convention structure does to the organization of campaigns, it is clear that it considerably reduces the relative weight of the party establishment in the selection of the new leader. Ian Stewart (1988) has argued that party elites often have different interests and candidates in national leadership selection contests and it is likely the same is true in provincial conventions. In a province like British Columbia with strong populist impulses this turns out (as we note below) to be important.

Social Credit is, without much doubt, the most populist of the three parties. We have seen this in the attitudes of its activists and it shows up sharply in the party's organization. For instance it has the most straightforward convention structure. There are no delegate categories other than elected constituency representatives and all constituencies are entitled to send the same number (25) of delegates. The rules actually provide that constituencies with extraordinarily large memberships have a few more delegates but only seven of the fifty associations qualified in 1986. The constitution provides that MLAS are to be treated no differently than regular party members and must seek election like all other delegates. This is a structure that seems designed to minimize the impact of the party's elected politicians. In fact the 1986 convention organizing committee, fearing some of their MLAS might be embarrassed by being defeated in an open party meeting of their local associations, ruled that they were to be automatically included in the constituency's delegation.

Party conventions, organized around constituency associations, are inevitably influenced in important and often unheralded ways by the character and shape of a province's constituency map. In the case of Social Credit, this was to be particularly important. In 1986, British Columbia had one of the most malapportioned electoral maps in the country coupled with a number of double-member ridings. This meant that the non-metropolitan areas were grossly over-represented, since all the double-member ridings were in the urban core of the province. And the party's rules do not provide that they should have double representation at a convention. Given that there was a pronounced regional dimension to candidate support patterns (Chapter 8), this structural feature may have had an impact on the outcome of the convention. Thus our calculations suggest that had double-member ridings been given double the standard number of delegates, the Vancouver area favourite candidate, Grace McCarthy, who was in second place on the first ballot, would have had a vote share that was a few per cent higher than she actually won. Whether this would have changed the dynamics of the convention is problematic: certainly it could not have hurt her.

It may well be that considerations of this sort lay at the heart of some of the conflict within Social Credit over reforming the electoral map. After a prolonged legal challenge to the malapportioned map, in 1989 the Supreme Court of British Columbia declared the current map violated the Canadian Charter of Rights and ordered that reapportionment be done promptly, implying that a plus or minus 25 per cent standard would be one acceptable norm. The Fisher Royal Commission, set up by the Vander Zalm government to eliminate dual member ridings, had produced such a plan and, after the court decision, it was adopted by the legislature. With this electoral map, the lower mainland area (greater Vancouver) will go from having about 30 per cent to some 42 per cent of the delegates at a Social Credit convention if the party maintains its current constitution and rules. Thus, more than anything else, constituency reform has the potential to alter dramatically the distribution and structure of power within Social Credit (or any other territorially structured party) and the outcome of future leadership contests.

Despite their inclusion of delegates from affiliated organizations (largely trade unions), New Democratic conventions are also dominated by constituency delegates. However, the New Democrats reject territorial representation. They operate not in terms of equal representation for constituency associations per se but on the principal that it is individual party members who ought to be equally represented. The result is that local party associations with large memberships have more delegates than those with small ones. In practice, this means the largest (in terms of numbers of members) constituency can send several times as many delegates to a provincial leadership convention as can the smallest. In 1987, this meant that about 45 per cent of the delegates to the convention that selected Harcourt leader came from NDP-held constituencies though these constituted but 35 per cent of the province's constituencies (with 30 per cent of the seats). In effect, this is a structure which tends to reinforce the existing balance of forces within the party for it is especially difficult for outsiders or new interests to penetrate the convention through mobilizing support in weakly-organized constituencies.

Given the weakness of the Liberal party in the province's politics, many of the delegates to its 1987 convention were primarily interested in federal politics. Thus 77 per cent of them said they thought federal politics is more important than provincial (as compared to just 40 per cent of the New Democrats), and fully 40 per cent reported having been at the 1984 convention that chose John Turner for national leader. The constituency delegates were almost evenly divided between those from federal and provincial associations, providing the one significant institutional cleavage in the convention. Had the leadership ultimately been contested, such a division might well have provided a important basis for internal party conflict.

The third distinctive characteristic of these provincial conventions is the long record of political activism of the delegates observed in Chapters 2 and 3. About half the delegates had joined their party before Bill Bennett defeated the NDP and polarized political choice in the province. They have served on constituency association executives, raised money for their party and its candidates, attended previous party conventions, and worked in recent general elections. Most see themselves as part of the 'party's central group in [their] constituency' and are active in the local politics of their home community (Table 23).

TABLE 23

Partisan activity among BC leadership convention delegates
(percentages)

	Social Credit	NDP	Liberal
Joined before 1975	51.7	45.8	48.9
Constituency executive member (past or present)	60.0	72.1	63.3
Helped raise funds for party	66.8	87.4	73.3
Attended an annual party convention	66.8	70.2	
Worked in campaign for party candidate	83.5	98.9	84.4
Part of central group in constituency	77.1	75.1	
Actively involved in local politics	65.0	68.4	42.7

On balance, these convention delegates are individuals who have a well developed understanding of their party and the individuals who offer to lead them. It may well be that such delegates are less likely to be impressed or persuaded by elaborate leadership campaigns than are the rather less politically experienced delegates who win the right to attend national party leadership selection conventions. There is some evidence of this among our Social Credit respondents. Half of them reported that they decided who they intended to support as soon as their preferred candidate announced his or her intention to run. Most clearly disapproved of the expensive conventioneering: almost two-thirds responded that they thought too much money had been spent by some of the candidates and more than half decided they want the party to put limits on leadership campaign expenditures in the future.

Taken together, these features generate a portrait of smaller, simpler conventions that are dominated by active and knowledgeable partisans. In this sense they come much closer than national conventions to representing the working core of the respective parties.

THREE LEADERSHIP CONTESTS

Between the summer of 1986 and the fall of 1987, the British Columbia Social Credit, New Democratic, and Liberal parties held leadership selection conventions and chose new leaders. Social Credit started the process when its leader (and the premier) Bill Bennett surprised his cabinet, his caucus, his party, and the province with his resignation.

The result was the most contested party leadership selection convention in Canadian history. Twelve individuals sought the job: cabinet ministers (current and former), backbench MLAs, municipal and federal politicians, aides to the outgoing leader, and a former minister who had abandoned his colleagues three years previously and had refused to run in the 1983 provincial election. This dissident ex-minister, Bill Vander Zalm, won on the fourth ballot. At the time of the leadership convention, Social Credit was unpopular, in part because of the extraordinary controversy and conflict that the government's post-1983 election program of neo-conservative social and economic policies had produced. Vander Zalm proved to be an extremely popular choice: within a couple of months he called a snap election and rode a populist wave back to office with an enhanced majority. As it happened the nature and size of his victory was misunderstood and exaggerated by the media. The increased majority was principally an artifact of a larger legislative assembly. His vote share was not significantly different from that won by Bennett in previous Social Credit wins.

In an election focused almost entirely on personality and leadership, as 1986 was, the New Democrats were in a weak position. With former premier Dave Barrett's resignation in 1984 they had, in a brokered but very competitive convention, compromised on a quiet, unassuming backbench MLA named Bob Skelly. He had been in third place on the first ballot but had outlasted his more popular rivals to win on a fifth ballot. It was victory in which the trade unionists were believed to have combined with the party's left to deny the leadership to a candidate (David Vickers) who obviously represented the new professional, urban, middle class activists that had been swelling the party ranks over the previous decade. Skelly never mastered the mass media, which was, in any event, entranced with Vander Zalm. The result was a disastrous campaign and the New Democrats lost the election that only months before they had confidently expected to win. In the aftermath Skelly resigned and only Michael Harcourt, former mayor of Vancouver and a newly elected MLA, contested the leadership at the 1987 annual party convention. His acclamation was marked by some with enthusiasm, by others with a sense of the inevitable.

The Liberals too faced a leadership convention in 1987 with the resignation of their leader, Art Lee, a former Vancouver Member of Parliament who had won considerable respect for his fight in the 1986 provincial election. Although he had not won a seat in the legislature, the party's vote had more than doubled (to 6.7%) and many thought this augured well for the party in the coming federal election. Several prominent BC Liberals were approached but none were willing to assume the thankless burdens of the provincial leadership. By the time of the convention, only Gordon Wilson, the Liberal candidate who had won the highest vote in the preceding election, let his name stand and was acclaimed.

The presence of twelve candidates assured that the leadership contest in Social Credit would expose its internal conflicts. But with no formal contests in either the NDP or the Liberal parties, the character of divisions over leadership must be assessed indirectly. We did ask delegates to both of those conventions if there was someone other than Harcourt or Wilson they would have preferred as leader, and if so who. Twenty-five per cent of the New Democrats said yes (and supplied other names); 39 per cent of the Liberals did likewise. In our analysis of leadership choice in the NDP and the Liberal party those two groups of delegates are taken to represent the new leaders' opposition within their respective parties. In the case of Social Credit we focus on the basic division between the final contenders, Vander Zalm and Brian Smith, as it appeared on the convention's decisive ballot. In the next chapter we present a detailed analysis of the Social Credit contest.

LEADERSHIP CHOICE IN THE PARTIES

To come immediately to the central question that we asked about party leadership selection in British Columbia we argue that the second of our two scenarios holds in all three cases. All the contests were free of any significant ideological dimension: other elements of party life dominated the process as the parties appeared to maintain an ideological unity in the face of their partisan enemies.

The Social Credit leadership contest was held at a time when the party was trailing in a number of public opinion polls. Normally a confident governing party, it had become perceived as arbitrary, distant, and too right-wing. Many of the delegates echoed this dissatisfaction with the leadership. Over 60 per cent of them agreed with the proposition that 'in recent years the party leader has been cut off too much from the opinions of ordinary party members'; over half said they thought the government's restraint program was 'not well implemented.' As the convention approached it was clear that the party had enthusiastically embraced a theme of renewal.

The basic division in the party seems to have ultimately rested on a split between insiders and outsiders. Five cabinet ministers were seeking to replace Bennett but so were seven other individuals. While the ministers were all obviously and inevitably associated with the government's record, the outsiders were able to establish

some distance. Bill Vander Zalm, in particular, was publicly ambivalent about the government's restraint program. The depth of this
division could be seen on the floor of the convention by the last
ballot. All of the ministerial candidates who crossed the floor went
to fellow minister Brian Smith who had virtually all the rest of the
cabinet (and the great majority of the caucus) with him. But of the
non-ministerial candidates, all but two (a federal Tory MP and a
Bennett aide) went to outsider Vander Zalm. The delegates response
to their elected leaders could be seen in the successive ballots. On
only one (the third) did the cabinet ministers together manage to
win even half the vote. This was a convention determined to repudiate the party's leadership and install a different political order.

Despite this rift in the party, and that considerable divergence of
opinion that we have seen exists on a wide range of policy alternatives, ideological factors did not constitute a significant determinant
of leadership choice on the final ballot. Vander Zalm delegates were
significantly more populist in their orientations than were Smith
voters (see Table 29 in the next chapter), further evidence of the
grassroots character of the insurgents' attack on their leadership. As
we shall see in detail in Chapter 8, there were powerful and significant regional effects at work in structuring delegate choice and long
serving party members especially preferred Vander Zalm, who hark-
ened back to the style of W.A.C. Bennett. In effect, Bill Bennett's new,
modernized party establishment lost control and was displaced by a
convention determined to recapture and restore its party.

The New Democrats were meeting to choose their new leader in
the aftermath of an election defeat which was widely regarded as a
personal triumph for the Social Credit leader but also as a decisive
repudiation of Skelly. New Democrats recognized the problem: 87
per cent of the NDP delegates thought that leadership had been an
important or very important element in their defeat. The party was
demoralized and realized that it too needed renewal: there was no
one in the caucus who was perceived as a credible leader capable of
competing with Vander Zalm. No established federal New Democratic politician was prepared to run and Mike Harcourt, who had
defeated Vander Zalm in a Vancouver mayoralty election, easily
emerged as the only candidate.

Still, a quarter of the delegates opposed his becoming leader, at
least to the extent of indicating they preferred someone else as party
leader. This division in the convention did not follow any of the
traditional left/right ideological cleavages that structure most internal policy debate in the social democratic party. The division
appears to have been much more strongly related to both tactical

questions and organizational features of the party.

In terms of the former, when asked 'What in your opinion is the most important issue facing the British Columbia New Democratic party today?' delegates provided us with a wide variety of responses covering two dozen topics. These party priorities can, however, be collapsed into two broad but distinctive categories: three-quarters of the delegates believed the most important issues were questions of leadership, public relations, and winning the next election; the other quarter pointed to policy concerns. This is the tension between the electoral pragmatists and the policy-oriented activists that long characterized the CCF/NDP (Young 1969). Our data show that the group we call the pragmatists were significantly more favourable to Harcourt's leadership than were those primarily concerned with policy. Those concerned with winning an election embraced Harcourt, despite (or perhaps because of) his public image as a moderate, reformist politician.

Two other bases for division over Harcourt's leadership can be seen in the data. Though delegates in all regions of the province supported him, there were some significant regional variations in the strength of the NDP winner's support. Curiously enough, the area where his opposition was strongest was his own supposed political base, the lower mainland. It is not clear how these variations are to be explained though they may reflect informal organizational networks in the party. One group that does stand out as more opposed to Harcourt's leadership is what we might call the party establishment (Table 24). Delegates who were at the convention by virtue of their membership on the provincial executive, or the party's federal or provincial councils were clearly at odds with individual party members. Although the numbers involved here are very small, the individuals themselves come from an important and powerful group in the party.

TABLE 24
Support for Harcourt by delegate status
(horizontal percentages)

	Yes	No	N
Constituency delegate	74.7	25.3	312
Affiliated member	64.3	35.7	28
Executive/council member	33.3	66.7	9
Elected politicians	100.0		9
All delegates	73.5	26.5	358

Thus the NDP delegates, like their Social Credit counterparts, seem to have been somewhat at odds with the organizational leadership of their party. The legislative caucus accepted Harcourt's leadership with little question but there is some indication (beyond the hint in Table 23) that the extra-parliamentary party establishment did not. The party executive rejected Harcourt's initial choice for party secretary, straining relationships between the party headquarters in Vancouver and the leader's office in Victoria. Harcourt responded by hiring an Ottawa civil servant to run his office, in effect trying to circumvent his opponents. That arrangement did not work. Harcourt had to fire him, which led to a civil suit for wrongful dismissal.

The Liberal leadership convention was marked by none of these divisions between the grassroots and the party establishment. Although the party sees its role as important in offering a moderate alternative to provincial voters, and in maintaining an organization to fight elections in what they see as the more important (by more than 3 to 1) federal arena, only 5 per cent of the activists at the leadership selection convention thought they had a high chance of winning their local constituency battle in the next provincial election. In that situation, the provincial leadership is hardly a prize to be fought over, certainly not one to divide the party in any systematic way. Liberals were happy enough to have a respectable candidate to take on the job.

CONCLUSION

This portrait of British Columbia's party activists engaged in the critical task of choosing new leaders suggests that the clash of ideologies that drives inter-party debate and electoral competition is not central to the competition for power and authority *within* the parties. It is as if the partisans were determined to maintain a façade of ideological unity in the face of the opposition. They do not expose any internal differences, any evidence of ideological disunity or disagreement, that might be exploited by the competition. The Liberals, who take pride in the fact that they reject the very polarization of politics that animates the system, did not divide at all.

But the populist style of politics practised in the province has its own impact on the system. Less than half the delegates in the two big parties disagreed with the proposition that their leader had been cut off from ordinary members. And when it came time to choose a new leader both groups elected a man who was at best distant from the existing party establishment. In the case of the more populist of the two parties, the Socreds, the repudiation of the party elite was most obvious and most direct. In the New Democratic party, the elite was apparently unable to put up its own candidate and thus had to accept the man their members had fixed upon.

It is assumed that these leaders will carry the ideological battle to the opposition and that there is no doubt about the lines of that conflict. Yet such leaders must be able to assert their authority, and come to command their party's elite, if they are to be successful. Vander Zalm began the process with his quick electoral victory but the subsequent rapid collapse of public confidence in his government put his leadership under considerable stress. When it became clear by late 1989 that he would have difficulty re-establishing his popularity, the party establishment signalled its discontent and four backbenchers resigned from the caucus. Following his party's sixth straight by-election loss, Vander Zalm appeared ready to resign as party leader. Instead, after keeping the party and the province in suspense for five weeks, he announced his determination to stay on, throwing down the gauntlet to those who sought to remove him.

Harcourt had difficulties with the elected executive of his party, but the party's electoral history and organizational traditions are such that he is not so likely to be openly challenged if he does not win. On the other hand, the speed with which Skelly left after the 1986 defeat indicates that NDP activists are not so tolerant as they once were of leaders who lose.

Finally, it is important to note that the divisions we observed in both parties were intimately related to the structure and size of the selection conventions. This leads us to argue that a change in the rules or organization of the party conventions might make a considerable difference to the outcome. A different electoral map, or a more typical representation of the party's elite in the process, would produce a different Social Credit leadership. For the New Democrats, organizational divisions can produce the sort of third choice that Skelly's leadership represented. If we are to come to a fuller understanding of these parties, and how they order British Columbia's politics, we must move beyond the ideological sound and fury to a concern for more institutional questions of organization and activity. We can see some of these forces at work in a detailed analysis of the Social Credit leadership struggle.

CHAPTER EIGHT

The Social Credit Grassroots Recapture Their Party

Social Credit activists participated in one of the most dramatic leadership selection contests in Canadian political history in 1986. As we noted in the last chapter, the result was to repudiate Bill Bennett's leadership style and his attempts to modernize the party organization. Bill Vander Zalm's victory ultimately represented the recapturing of Social Credit by those party activists who yearned for a return to the original populist party of W.A.C. Bennett. In this chapter, we are able to use the data from the Social Credit convention delegate survey to analyze the dynamics of this internal struggle for the soul of the governing party.

The Social Credit leadership contest was only the second in the party's history. The winner would become both the first non-Bennett to lead the party and the province's premier. The contest was precipitated by the unexpected resignation of Bill Bennett, who knew that his party lagged behind the New Democrats in the polls and that he himself was even less popular than his party. Still, the premier's decision was a shock. Though the majority of the activists thought his governing style remote, there had been no significant challenges to his leadership and there was no obvious successor poised to act.

The battle for succession in the party involved subtle and sometimes not so subtle efforts by many candidates to distance themselves from Bennett and the record of his government. Observers of the contest not only saw the distancing by many candidates from the incumbent leader, they also saw a struggle for control of the party between advocates of closer ties to the Progressive Conservative party and those wishing to preserve the tradition of federal neutrality; between the inheritors of the party's populist tradition and modern organization men and women; and between neo-conservatives and centrists.

THE CONTEST

Social Credit activists were presented with an extraordinary contest. The average number of candidates in conventions that have chosen premiers is under four and only once in Canadian history has there been one with more than six contestants (James 1987). In this contest a full dozen emerged. Something of the politically disparate character of the contest can be seen in the backgrounds of the twelve candidates who chose to contest the leadership: five (Grace McCarthy, Jim Nielson, Bill Ritchie, Stephen Rogers, and Brian Smith) had been long-serving members of the government though one (Stephen Rogers) had just left office under a conflict-of-interest cloud; two (Cliff Michael and John Reynolds) were backbench MLAS who hoped the convention would recognize abilities the premier had overlooked; another two (Kim Campbell and Bud Smith) were closely associated with the premier having worked in his office; one (Bob Wenman) was a federal Progressive Conservative MP who had served originally as a Social Credit MLA in the W.A.C. Bennett years; one (Mel Couvelier) was the mayor of a suburb of Victoria; and the last one, William Vander Zalm, was in private business. In his period as a Social Credit minister, Vander Zalm had served in three portfolios but on leaving politics the signals he gave publicly suggested a dislike for what the government and his colleagues were about.

The pre-convention campaign structure and organization were somewhat different from that which has characterized recent national leadership contests. This was a consequence of the brief duration (two months) of the campaign, and the abbreviated period within which constituencies had to choose delegates. Candidates had little opportunity to build organizations that could effectively influence the choice of delegates and they had to concentrate on exploiting the networks of friends and colleagues they already had in the party. Hence a high proportion of delegates report commitments made to the candidate personally. One delegate when asked to whom he had made his commitment answered 'Patrick Kinsella,' a reference to one of the country's best-known Conservative political strategists and an organizer of Brian Smith's campaign.

For all the apparent competition and choice implied by a field of twelve candidates, early in the campaign it became clear that there were four competitive candidates – McCarthy, the two (unrelated) Smiths, and Vander Zalm. On the first ballot the big four captured 78 per cent of the vote, leaving the rest spread across the eight others. None of the minor candidates won more than 54 votes (out of a total of 1294) and all lost their deposits. Six of these candidates immediately dropped out of the race. The second and third ballots effectively eliminated two of the major candidates, Bud Smith and Grace McCarthy respectively, leaving Vander Zalm to win on the fourth (Table 25).

TABLE 25
1986 Social Credit convention results

Candidate	Ballot number			
	1	2	3	4
Vander Zalm	367	457	625	801
Brian Smith	196	255	342	454
McCarthy	244	280	305	
Bud Smith	202	219		
Reynolds	54	39		
Nielson	54	30		
Rogers	43			
Wenman	40			
Michael	32			
Ritchie	28			
Couvelier	20			
Campbell	14			
Total	1294	1280	1272	1255

The four leading candidates couched their appeals in significantly different ways. The two Smiths were closely identified with premier Bennett and his attempt to build a party machine using all the expertise and technology of modern electoral politics. Their supporters were far more willing to approve of the use of professional organizers, modern advertising techniques and polls, as well as Bennett's party leadership style than were those of either McCarthy or Vander Zalm. Of the two, Brian Smith was the solid reliable insider portrayed as the man with the weight to be taken seriously as a premier; Bud Smith was the modern new man who offered a fresh face, never having run for office, but with wide experience of government and party. They both ran sophisticated campaigns directed by men well versed in leadership wars and Progressive Conservative electoral politics in other provinces as well as national-level contests.

Most observers expected that these organizational affinities would bring them together by the last ballot. Grace McCarthy ran on her record as party saviour during the dark years of the NDP government, her experience as a senior minister, and her well-known enthusiasm and positive 'put BC first' message. Though she continually denigrated the professional outsiders working for the Smiths, she had such help herself. Incorporating both federal Liberal and Conservative supporters she ran the slickest and costliest campaign. All of these three candidates put on very expensive campaigns that stood out well beyond anything ever seen in the province. The delegates noticed and reacted against the spending extravaganzas. Almost two-thirds of the delegates agreed that 'some candidates spent too much money on their campaigns' and 57 per cent agreed that the party ought to put limits on campaign expenditures. It is not surprising that the Smiths' supporters were less likely (and Vander Zalm's more likely) to agree with these propositions than delegates as a whole. Vander Zalm, on the other hand, who only entered the race five weeks before the convention ran an amateurish-looking, populist campaign promising simple government, fewer experts, more consultation with the people, and basic values. Inevitably, given the candidate, the Vander Zalm campaign centred almost entirely on his personality.

The personalistic anti-establishment campaign run by Vander Zalm meant that he had to reach around the party's elected elite to appeal to delegates directly. Most MLAs opposed him and by the final ballot were standing with their colleague Brian Smith. Of the activists who reported that they had made a convention vote commitment to their local MLA, there was a significant preference for Smith over Vander Zalm. The problem for the caucus was that the structure and norms of the party made it difficult for them to command such commitments. Only 9 per cent of the Social Credit delegates who committed themselves did so to their MLA. As a result, the caucus was given a leader most of it manifestly opposed.

As we also observed in the last chapter, the leadership campaigns also differed in their geographic reach. Not only did most minor candidates have geographically limited support (typically they won the support of the delegates from their home constituency and added to that scattered support of a personal kind), but there was also a pronounced regional bias to the support bases of three of the leaders (Table 26). Brian Smith won almost half his first ballot support from a Vancouver Island base that included his home riding of Victoria; Vancouver's Grace McCarthy had her base in the lower mainland; while Bud Smith (who was from Kamloops) depended heavily on an interior base. But none of those regions was large enough to dominate the others. Only Vander Zalm was able to command significant support in every region of the province. Only he won delegate support from more than half the ridings – 64 per cent of them. Grace McCarthy won delegates from half the constituencies; all the rest from far fewer. Not being a regionally defined candidate made it much easier for Vander Zalm to assemble a winning coalition as the balloting went on.

TABLE 26
First ballot support by region
(horizontal percentages)

Candidate	Island	Lower Mainland	Fraser Valley	Kootenay	Interior/ Okanagan	North/ Peace River
McCarthy	15.3	52.5	0.0	6.8	16.9	8.5
Brian Smith	47.8	10.9	0.0	17.4	15.2	8.7
Bud Smith	10.5	10.5	0.0	7.9	44.7	26.3
Vander Zalm	17.0	27.0	9.0	13.0	27.0	7.0
Total	22.5	31.1	4.3	10.2	21.8	10.2

This important regional dimension of the contest coloured the course of the convention and helped shape its final outcome. Bud Smith was always in the most difficult position for not only was his base region the smallest, but some two-thirds of the eight minor candidates' support was located in either the Island or the lower mainland. That made it particularly hard for him to compete with either Brian Smith or McCarthy for the second preferences of those activists and he found himself in fourth place on the second ballot. As a result, he was forced out of the contest. On the other hand, the lack of a regional cast to his support apparently placed Vander Zalm in the best position to attract second preferences. This can be seen in the delegates who moved between the first and second ballots: few who moved to McCarthy or Brian Smith were from Bud Smith's Central Interior/Okanagan bailiwick but a quarter of those going to Vander Zalm were. Once Bud Smith was forced out of the race, that trickle became a torrent.

As the convention moved from ballot to ballot, as candidates dropped out and moved to support others, and as the results altered their realistic choices, large numbers of delegates had to rethink their votes. The data indicate that about a quarter of the delegates changed their vote between any two successive ballots. If one's candidate was still in the race, the question was whether to *stay* or to *abandon*. If one's candidate had dropped off the ballot the question was whether to *follow* his or her lead or to *flee* to another candidate. Although the numbers abandoning their candidate dropped sharply as the convention moved on, as the distance between ballots increased, the proportion still supporting their original candidate had to decline. In the end, just over 40 per cent voted the same way on the first and last ballots. Given the numbers involved, the decisions by individual delegates became especially salient when Bud Smith dropped out of the race on the second ballot and turned not to Brian Smith, as many had predicted, but walked to the Vander Zalm camp. On the last ballot the McCarthy supporters did not have this choice to follow or flee as they had been left on their *own*. The pattern of delegates' ballot movement in the convention is reported in Table 27. For example, between the first and second ballots 75.5 per cent of delegates stayed with their first choice when that candidate remained in the race, but 8.9 per cent shifted to another candidate. A further 15.8 per cent of the delegates (the sum of columns 3 and 4) had to choose a different candidate because their first ballot choice was no longer available. Slightly more of them, a total of 9.3 per cent of the sample, voted for someone other than the candidate preferred by the person they supported on the first ballot.

TABLE 27
Delegate movement between ballots
(horizontal percentages)

Ballots	Candidate IN		Candidate OUT			
	stay	abandon	follow	flee	own	
1 -> 2	75.5	8.9	6.6	9.3		(337)
2 -> 3	76.0	6.3	12.8	5.0		(336)
3 -> 4	77.5	2.7			19.7	(330)
1 -> 3	59.0	4.2	21.9	15.0		(335)
2 -> 4	57.6	4.5	13.5	4.5	19.9	(332)
1 -> 4	43.5	2.4	25.6	11.7	16.6	(331)

NOTE: Cell entries are percentages of the entire convention voting in the indicated pair of ballots. The own category contains third ballot McCarthy supporters who were forced to make up their own minds because McCarthy did not make her fourth ballot preference public.

Those delegates freed because their previous choice is no longer on the ballot constitute special prizes available for convention strategists and are the stuff of endless strategy and detailed tactics. Amongst Socred delegates one pattern stands out. Delegates freed early in the convention (after the first ballot) were more likely to flee than follow their candidate's signal, while the reverse was true for those released later in the process. That pattern makes political sense. Many of the minor candidates won a promise of first ballot support but their delegates fully expected to move on the second ballot and had decided who to vote for on their own.[1] This was less likely true for delegates who were supporting major candidates and expected their favourite to be on the final ballot.

An examination of the patterns of delegate vote-shifting in Table 28 reveals some interesting variations amongst the several camps. Of the six candidates who dropped out after the first ballot only two, Rogers and Wenman, managed to carry a majority of supporters with them to their preferred candidate.[2] Rogers had made it clear during the campaign that he could not live with a Vander Zalm leadership and our survey only turned up one Rogers delegate who voted for the winner on any ballot (and that the last). By contrast Campbell, Couvelier, Michael, and Ritchie supporters paid little attention to what their candidates did and scattered their votes among the remaining candidates. The pattern of those abandoning Nielson and Reynolds after the first ballot was similar. Those delegates appear to have gone in all directions, each of the major candidates winning some, but none of them winning a majority.

Delegate movement after the second ballot was clearly quite a different story. As the table indicates, the great majority of them went with their candidate. What remains to be discovered is whether those delegates followed their candidate or whether both were naturally going in the same direction.

In an attempt to answer this question, we asked the delegates if their candidate's crossing of the floor influenced their later votes. Of those who answered, one quarter said yes. (Sixty-two per cent of the first ballot voters never saw their candidate endorse another one.) By sheer weight of numbers the bulk of those who were swayed (some 58%) were necessarily Bud Smith voters. More interestingly, of the nine camps, only in Bud Smith's did those claiming to be influenced outnumber those who said they were not. Can we conclude from this that Smith's dramatic and unexpected crossing of the floor to Vander Zalm was a critical and decisive event in the evolution of the Social Credit party? The answer appears to be a simple no. It is true that 74 per cent of those Smith delegates who said they were influ-

TABLE 28
Delegate movement by candidate
(horizontal percentages)

Candidate	moved to	Supporters		
		follow	flee	
Ballots 1 -> 2				
Campbell	Brian Smith	25.0	75.0	(8)
Couvelier	Vander Zalm	37.5	62.5	(8)
Michael	Reynolds		100.0	(4)
Ritchie	Brian Smith	16.7	83.3	(6)
Rogers	Brian Smith	53.8	46.2	(13)
Wenman	Brian Smith	64.3	35.7	(14)
Ballots 2 -> 3				
Nielson	Brian Smith	80.0	20.0	(5)
Reynolds	Vander Zalm	62.5	37.5	(8)
Bud Smith	Vander Zalm	72.3	17.6	(47)

enced by him voted for Vander Zalm on the third ballot, but then so did 71 per cent of those who claimed his action did not affect them. There is not much support for an argument that the candidate made a significant difference here. Smith himself publicly claimed to be going where the convention (and his delegates) wanted to go.

This pattern leads us to believe that once the balloting started the candidates' endorsements had little impact. The delegates knew who they wanted to win and, having cast their first vote for a host of personal and other local reasons, moved directly to their real choice. At this point then, the question is whether the various attitudinal dimensions that divide the party can help us to account for these real choices or whether it was nothing more than a geographically structured personality contest.

EXPLAINING THE DELEGATES' FINAL CHOICE

Given the divisions of opinion among delegates and differences among the candidates in the degree to which they were associated with the Bennett administration, differences in campaign styles, and reputed policy differences, one would expect to see some relationship between delegate opinions and their final choices. Table 29 provides information on these relationships by looking at the profile of each of the principal contender's supporters on the final three ballots. For this we utilize the attitude scales developed in Chapter 4 to map the opinions and values of Social Credit activists. The first thing to note is that significant differences appear between groups of supporters on every dimension except continentalism. (On the second ballot, differences on the collectivism/individualism scale were only significant to 0.10) In every case and on all ballots, the supporters of Bill Vander Zalm exhibit attitudes which place them on high end of each of the scales. Thus, they are the most populist, most individualistic, most supportive of restraint, and most hostile to government regulation. The results on the pro-restraint scale seem incongruous since Vander Zalm publicly opposed what were considered to be excesses of the restraint program during his bid for the leadership, whereas Grace McCarthy and Brian Smith were prominent members of the government which implemented it.

TABLE 29
Attitude scale scores by leadership choice

		Leadership Vote				
Attitude scale	(Ballot)	Bud Smith	Grace McCarthy	Brian Smith	Bill Vander Zalm	Sig. level
Continentalism	(2)	2.22	2.27	2.25	2.36	.68
	(3)		2.16	2.31	2.38	.16
	(4)			2.38	2.28	.32
Collective versus	(2)	3.69	3.46	3.62	3.95	.09
individual	(3)		3.41	3.57	3.93	.01
responsibility	(4)			3.45	3.87	.01
Populism	(2)	2.06	2.28	2.06	2.64	<.01
	(3)		2.20	1.95	2.55	.02
	(4)			1.88	2.54	<.01
Pro-restraint	(2)	2.26	2.34	2.36	3.10	<.01
	(3)		2.35	2.21	2.88	.01
	(4)			2.07	2.88	<.01
Anti-regulation	(2)	2.25	2.24	2.15	2.49	.01
	(3)		2.23	2.12	2.45	<.01
	(4)			2.11	2.43	<.01

NOTE: Cell entries are scale score means. For details of scale construction see Appendix. Total Ns differ given varying amounts of missing data. Ns by candidate and ballot for the collective versus individual responsibility scale are Bud Smith (36), Grace McCarthy (48, 46), Brian Smith (52, 61, 71), and Bill Vander Zalm (97, 131, 166).

The general pattern with respect to the other three candidates' supporters was more mixed. Looking at the second ballot, it appears the two Smiths' supporters were similar on both the individualism and populism scales: they were less populist and more individualist than were McCarthy's. On the other two scales, the Bud Smith group was less supportive of restraint than were the other two groups but more opposed to government regulation. McCarthy and Brian Smith supporters were virtually the same in their views on restraint but on regulation Smith's group were less opposed than those of McCarthy. On the third ballot, McCarthy's supporters remained intermediate between those of Vander Zalm and Brian Smith on populism and opposition to regulation and to the left of Smith supporters on collective versus individual responsibility. Now, however, McCarthy's group was somewhat more supportive of the restraint program than was Smith's.

At first glance then, Social Credit activists appear to have clearly divided in terms of their ideological preferences. But notwithstanding these persistent differences linked to policy (evident in Table 29), when we examine the simultaneous effect of attitudinal variables, taking into account other features of candidate followings already discussed, a rather different picture emerges. Most policy differences recede into the background as we attempt to account for third and fourth ballot choices.

This conclusion is based on the analysis reported in Table 30. The third ballot offered three pairs of comparisons between delegates – McCarthy supporters versus Vander Zalm's, Vander Zalm's versus Brian Smith's, and Brian Smith's versus McCarthy's. The fourth ballot, with only two contenders still in the race, offered one pair. Using regression analysis we can identify what delegate characteristics (political attitudes, region, etc.) were associated with a choice of one candidate over another.[3] The R^2 figures at the bottom of each column measure how much of the difference between groups of delegates is explained by the characteristics listed in the column. Since R^2 has a possible range of 0 to 1, the figures reported in the table are of moderate size but comparable to what is typically found in this kind of analysis.

Each explanatory variable has a regression coefficient associated with it unless there was no statistically significant relationship. The sign of the coefficient tells us the direction of the relationship between a given characteristic and leadership choice. For variables such as duration of party membership, continentalism, and populism, this has a straightforward interpretation. A negative sign for membership duration means that a long-time party member is less likely than a newer member to be a supporter of the candidate whose name appears first in a given column. Similarly, negative signs for the two attitude scale variables tell us that high scorers on these scales are also less likely to prefer the first named candidate than low scorers.

Gender and the regional variables are dichotomies. In the case of male versus female, a negative sign indicates that males are less likely than females to support the first-named candidate. Each of the regional variables allows a comparison between delegates from the named region and those from the lower mainland. For example, the positive coefficient of 0.41 for the Island variable in the Brian Smith versus McCarthy column tells us that Island delegates were more likely to be Brian Smith supporters than those from the lower mainland even after we take gender, length of membership, and political attitudes into account.

The bottom line on McCarthy's supporters is that there were significantly more females, and they were less continentalist, less populist, and less likely to come from the Interior or the Okanagan than Vander Zalm supporters. The only policy differences which distinguished her supporters from those who voted for Brian Smith are those captured by the continentalism scale – his supporters were significantly more supportive of freer trade and less concerned about a possible loss of Canada's economic independence. But there were powerful regional differences associated with Brian Smith's greater appeal to delegates from the Kootenays and Vancouver Island. The result for continentalism is surprising given the lack of significant differences on this dimension reported in Table 29, but may be attributable to the overlap between support for continentalism and rejection of populist positions.

The contrast between Vander Zalm and Brian Smith supporters apparent on the third ballot – Smith's relative strength on Vancouver Island, and Vander Zalm's greater appeal to populists and long time party members – was carried through to the fourth and final ballot virtually unchanged.

Despite differences within the party on a variety of policy issues, particularly those linked to the implementation of the restraint program, the leadership aspirants appeared unwilling or unable to exploit these differences directly. They simply played no part in structuring the delegates' decisions as to who their next leader should be. Some of the minor candidates did try to develop distinctive issue-based support, but they lacked the regional base which proved necessary in order to challenge Vander Zalm at all. In the end, even a strong regional base was not sufficient to ensure victory.

The analysis summarized in Table 30 reveals that the struggle ultimately became one of ins versus outs, between party professionals and the long-serving grassroots, between non-populists and populists, and the latter won.

TABLE 30
Multiple determinants of leadership choice

THIRD BALLOT	McCarthy vs. Vander Zalm	Vander Zalm vs. Brian Smith	Brian Smith vs. McCarthy
Male vs. female	-.19 (1.76)	–	–
Duration of party membership	–	.08 (2.46)	–
Continentalism	-.18 (3.18)	–	.13 (1.85)
Populism	-.14 (1.72)	.16 (3.55)	–
Island	–	-.54 (5.51)	.41 (2.99)
Kootenay	–	–	.38 (1.84)
Interior/Okanagan	-.19 (1.83)	–	–
Constant	1.12 (5.21)	.14 (0.95)	.10 (0.55)
R^2	.19	.35	.22
FOURTH BALLOT			
Duration of party membership		.08 (2.64)	
Populism		.16 (3.81)	
Island		-.41 (4.54)	
Constant		.12 (0.99)	
R^2		.30	

NOTE: Table entries are regression coefficients with absolute values of the t-ratio in parentheses. The dependent variable in each model is given by the column heading with voters for the first candidate named scores '1' and the other candidate's supporters scored '0.' All coefficients are significant at the .05 level, one-tailed. Regional variables are dummy variables with the value '1' for all delegates from the designated region, '0' otherwise. Male vs. female is a dummy variable with males scored '1.' The populism and continentalism variables use scores from attitude scales described in the Appendix. The duration of membership variable is scored from 1 to 5 depending on whether the delegate joined the party in 1986, 1980-5, 1975-9, 1972-5, or before 1972, respectively.

Bill Vander Zalm promised a different style of leadership, but while different it was not new for many Social Credit activists. In appealing to populists suspicious of bureaucracy and impatient with delay, and long time party members, many of whom had been originally attracted to Social Credit during the W.A.C. Bennett era, Vander Zalm was offering a style with which they were familiar and comfortable. He may have been criticized by some delegates (and candidates) as well as the media for offering style rather than substance, but, given the ideological divisions in the party, a policy-oriented campaign would have made the road to victory much rougher. It would have exposed divisions within the party Social Credit would rather hide in the interests of electoral success.

CHAPTER NINE

Resisting Polarization:
The Survival of the Liberals

ROBYN A. SO WITH THE AUTHORS

Casual observers of BC politics are often surprised to learn that an active provincial Liberal party organization still exists. Fifty years ago, it dominated provincial politics, today it struggles to be noticed and taken seriously. Since the 1952 electoral debacle, when the decade old Liberal-Conservative coalition lost office to the Social Credit party, the Liberal's popularity has steadily declined: its vote collapsed in the 1975 election and then virtually disappeared in 1979. In the past three elections it has not managed to elect a single member to the legislature. Although its share of the popular vote rose in the 1986 election to just above 6 per cent, prospects for any substantial revival in the fortunes of the party remain bleak. Local political pundits readily dismiss the party as moribund. Its lack of recognizable candidates, the comparatively short tenure of its leaders, its lack of financial resources, and its thin organizational base merely reinforce the portrait of an unviable party.

Yet despite this sorry state the party has not disappeared from the provincial political stage as have the Progressive Conservatives. Indeed almost half (43%) its current activists joined the party since 1979. On the other hand, 40 per cent of active party members joined over fifteen years ago when they might plausibly have perceived the Liberal party as a viable electoral force. These individuals have stayed with the party through its darkest days. In the face of continuing provincial defeats, what underlies the motivations of these Liberals' continuing enthusiasm and longstanding partisan activity? As for the former, those who have joined more recently, what motivates them to join a party whose experience of governing is beyond the memory and experience of most British Columbians?

Conventional wisdom and a good deal of academic literature suggests that a cadre-type political party like the Liberals will attract activists only if they can be rewarded with victory, or at least the prospects of winning. Otherwise such a party ultimately loses its activists and thus its ultimate means of survival. Frank Sorauf (1964:81), among others, has argued that: 'if the party is to continue functioning as an organization it must make "payments" in an acceptable "political currency" adequate to motivate and allocate the labors of its workers.' And he goes on to observe that: 'For the party to maintain its reward system and produce payoffs on it, it must win elections ... Even ... social and psychological rewards depend ultimately on the party's maintaining status, voter clientele, and the exhilaration of victory' (89–90).

The logic is clear and simple: continuing electoral defeat will leave a party unable to reward, and thus hold, its activists. Without activists, a party cannot long survive as a viable independent political organization. The disappearance of British Columbia's provincial Conservative party appears to be an example of this dynamic.

Why then does anybody continue to work for the BC Liberal party given its manifest inability to satisfy its activists and supporters with electoral victory? Why are these British Columbians not working for the Social Credit or the New Democratic parties, both of which are more effective competitors able to offer their partisans the prospects of winning future general elections? One possible explanation, of course, is that winning is simply not as important to these activists as are other motivations. But if this is correct then Sorauf's assumption about the nature of organizational motivation in political parties is untenable, at least in British Columbia. Alternatively, it may be that Liberal activists actually believe, in spite of the present reality, that the party can and will win in future.

This chapter addresses the perplexing question of the survival of the BC Liberal party by examining the involvement and motivation of its activists. Our principal argument is that BC Liberal activists are inspired by a variety of motivations that are, in part, a reflection of British Columbia's partisan history and its bifurcated political world. The Liberal Party has remained a major player in national politics and this is not without consequence for many politically active British Columbians.

The literature on the motivations of individual party activists suggests that there are three dispositions that stimulate people to become politically active. These are commonly referred to as affective, material, and purposive incentives (Perlin 1980; Sorauf 1964). Affective incentives include those that satisfy social status and belonging needs; material ones refer to those that promise direct rewards, such as jobs or marketable benefits; while purposive incentives refer to personal commitments to an ideology, policy, or perhaps a politician. The fulfilment of individual activists' needs may depend on party success but in some instances it may also be quite independent of it. Certainly material rewards are likely to be produced by a winning party, and this is what led Sorauf to emphasize the need for cadre parties (like the Liberals) to win.

Since the British Columbia Liberal party does not win elections, we expect that activism must be largely governed by incentives satisfied independently of the party's provincial electoral record. One of the most important of these will likely be ideology for it has a capacity to tie an activist to a party independently of its worldly success, or lack of it. Not only do we expect that the personal beliefs and values of Liberals will be critical motivations but also that they will perceive their ideological perspectives as a distinctive element in an otherwise polarized BC party system. Thus politically interested British Columbians who reject the free enterprise/socialism polarization as defined by the two major parties, and who believe in principle that a moderate choice is necessary will make natural Liberal activists. This suggests that the Liberals – the classic brokerage politics cadre party – can endure provincially only by becoming ideologues of the centre. This is no easy task and may account for its very limited appeal.

Alan Abramowitz and his colleagues (1986:63), in a study of state party conventions in the United States, found that purposive incentives of this sort were reported as the most important motivations to party activism there and that 'personal benefits received from participation ... were rated much lower in importance [than purposive incentives] by delegates in both parties ... [Republicans and Democrats]' (64). They also found that purposive motivations were positively correlated with party loyalty, a relationship which would help explain long partisan service. The Liberals fit this mould.

We have already mapped out the distinctive policy and issue positions held by BC Liberal activists. These surely provide a substantive base for activists' perceptions that they do not fit in with the other two parties, either ideologically or in terms of specific issues or policy domains. Unfortunately our Liberal respondents were not queried directly as to their motivations for activism in the party. We have, therefore, no first order test for the relative importance of the three kinds of motivations that have been found to exist in other political parties. But in response to an open-ended question about why they first joined the party, only one Liberal activist spontaneously mentioned social factors such as fellowship and congeniality.

This is not to say that solidarity motivations and affective incentives are not an important element in governing activity in the provincial party, though it suggests they may be less important than other motivations. The largest group of Liberals report they are attracted to the party precisely because it has a centrist vocation.

THE VIEW FROM THE CENTRE

Liberal activists have a perception of the British Columbian party system that marks theirs out as a distinctive party, one quite apart from either the New Democrats or the Socreds. We presented Liberal delegates with a seven-point scale, with the ends labelled Left and Right, and asked them to locate each of the three parties on it. Whereas 95 per cent of our Liberals defined a range left of centre as the position occupied by the NDP, only 12 per cent of them put their own party in that same space (Figure 8). The Social Credit party was put within a range right of centre by all the respondents but only two per cent thought the Liberal Party belonged there. Fully 87 per cent of the Liberals placed their party either at the centre of the ideological scale or one point to the right. These Liberal activists clearly see their party as occupying a unique position in the party system and operating very much as a centrist alternative in an otherwise ideologically polarized electoral politics.

Liberals also explicitly define their party as one with a moderate ideology. To the question, 'Why are you a Liberal?,' 50 per cent of them responded with some variant of the idea that it was a 'moderate' party. When we add to those respondents activists who replied that the Liberal party's appeal for them was based on the fact that its policy stands were congruent with their personal beliefs we can account for almost three-quarters of the total.

By contrast, New Democratic and Social Credit party activists are less enthusiastic moderates, no doubt because they are less concerned about the consequences of polarization. Less than half of the NDP activists (44%) were prepared to agree with the proposition that their party had to be careful not to move too far to the left, and just more than half of the Socred activists (53%) thought moving too far right was a danger to the party. Those who are Liberal activists may be right: their party seems to be the obvious and most appropriate vehicle for those whose political avocation is determinedly moderate and, in their view of the political world, ideologically neutral.

As we saw in Chapter 6 for the most part this centrist orientation of Liberal activists is generally matched by their specific policy preferences. Liberal activists see this not as an unwillingness to take

FIGURE 8
Liberals' perception of party space

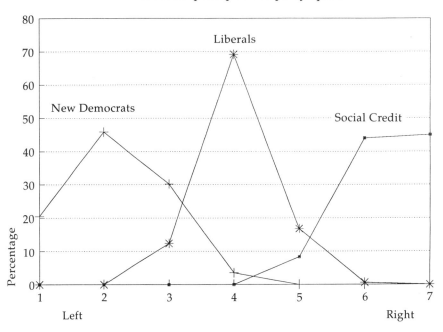

sides but as a positive virtue for they believe that the centre represents a distinctive and valued position in its own right.

OPTIMISTS OR REALISTS?

Notwithstanding this aggressive centrism among Liberals it must be
difficult to sustain activism in the face of the continued weak showing of the party in provincial elections. What we found, however,
was that in spite of its performance, this is a party in which many
members are persistently optimistic about its future: some go so far
as to expect that they could possibly form the government, and win
up to 55 per cent of the popular vote in the next election.

In our questionnaire activists were asked, 'What do you think are
realistic goals for the Liberal party in the next provincial election?'
and invited to respond both in terms of a popular vote share and
specific number of seats (up to opposition or government status) in
the legislature. Although targets of 30 per cent or more of the popular vote were given by only a minority of respondents (10.5%), it was
also the case that an equally small proportion predicted much more
realistic figures of 10 per cent or less. The median 'realistic goal' of

these activists was 19 per cent. This is in spite of the fact the party
has not been able to poll even half that per cent since 1972. This
optimism, coupled with their passion for a centre 'alternative' is a
big part of the story of why these individuals remain active provincial Liberals. And recent Liberals are no more or less optimistic than
veterans of fifteen years or more!

Where does this optimism come from? In a party as down as the
Liberals one of the most vital tasks of the leadership is to encourage
and bolster their troops. Thus it is to be expected that they will
easily exaggerate what the outcome of the last (1986) election fore-
shadows for the party. Given that this campaign led to an observ-
able increase in the Liberal's share of the vote for the first time in a
decade (a 150% increase from 2.7% to 6.7%), the literature produced
by the party elite for their activists attending the 1987 leadership
convention portrayed this outcome as a harbinger of good things to
come:

> the doubling of our vote in the provincial election proves to me that we
> can and will elect Liberals to the Legislature.[1]

> We didn't achieve the results we had hoped for during the last election by
> winning a seat, but we did manage to raise the profile of liberalism in BC
> That was evidenced by our percentage of the popular vote. The break-
> through we hope for will have to await another election and a new leader,
> but I know it will come. One day there will be a Liberal government in
> Victoria.[2]

> Art [Lee]'s tireless efforts during the last campaign resulted in the dou-
> bling of our popular vote and have provided the foundation upon which
> we can all build.[3]

> It is exciting to contemplate the rise in popularity of our party in British
> Columbia over the last two and one half years and its implications for our
> future. The recent provincial election showed us that people in this prov-
> ince are willing to take a second look at the Liberal alternative.[4]

> we were able to double our percentage of the popular vote in the 1986
> campaign. More people began to recognize the need for a moderate party
> of the centre.[5]

These assertions, which constituted the party leadership's claims to
further support and work from their activists, touched on a number
of themes. They repeatedly said that the party was on the rise, and
that this could be attributed to the efforts of Liberal workers. They
reasserted the proposition that the Liberal party was a moderate

centrist party and said that was precisely what the province needed. Given that aggressive centrism is what attracted many of these activists to the Liberal party such reassurances are vital to keeping them active.

Both the provincial and national leaders went on to promise that more effort would generate an even better showing in the next election. Thus Art Lee (the outgoing leader) said

> During the past two years, Liberals have all worked very hard to re-establish our Party as a political force in British Columbia. Although we were not successful in winning a seat in the recent general election, the Party did double its popular vote. Liberals can be very proud of this achievement, and because of our result at the polls, we also can be very optimistic about our future role in British Columbia.[6]

and John Turner (the national Liberal leader) wrote the provincial convention delegates that:

> I am convinced that we have what it takes to make great inroads in this province in the coming months. If we strengthen our resolve, discipline our efforts and unite in a common purpose, we will move quickly and surely towards a brighter future.[7]

All this is designed to reassure existing Liberals that activism in the party had meaning and utility. Hard work had paid off in the last election and therefore will in the next. All the messages are aimed at reinforcing optimism and reaffirming the province's need for a centrist political option.

But of course not all activists are Pollyanna optimists and it would be misleading to think that the party consists only of individuals who have an unrealistically rosy view of the future. There are many, perhaps even a majority, who have a more worldly view of electoral competition in the province, at least as it is played out in their community. To tap this element in the party we divided the activists into two groups which we have labelled *optimists* and *realists*. The partition is straightforward: an optimist is defined as an activist who rates the Liberals' chance of winning their local seat, at the next provincial election, as medium or high; a realist is one who rates the prospects as low or nonexistent. By this criterion, optimists constitute 45 per cent of our sample, the remainder are the realists.

The optimists tend to think Liberal success is largely dependent upon their efforts and, in general, factors which are within the control of the party. As a result they are more likely to rate their party's leader and platform, as opposed to a weak Social Credit or NDP, as important factors governing the outcome of electoral battles. Thus future victories are possible by successful manipulation of these variables and so, by implication, there is good reason to stay active, work hard, and be optimistic about the Liberal future in British Columbia. Realists, on the other hand, are more likely to believe factors external to the party are critical in explaining their electoral success or setbacks. Thus they are more likely to rate a weak Social Credit or NDP performance as the most important element affecting Liberal prospects. Realists may be described as under fewer illusions that they control their provincial political environment than are their optimistic fellow partisans. When asked why Liberal federal voters desert the party provincially, the realists are more likely to admit that they do not want to waste their vote while the optimists return to their internal party themes of party organization, leadership, or candidates.

But realists are also more likely to agree that the strength of the federal Liberal party is an important strategic factor influencing the chance of provincial success. There is an important clue in this: realists are more oriented to the federal party where they see greater possibilities for controlling their political destinies. Other variables being held constant, realists are more likely than optimists to feel closer to the federal party (43% versus 13%) and less likely than optimists to feel equally close to both levels of the party organization (43% versus 67%). Realists were also more likely to have served in the higher echelons of the national party's organization: they predominated among those who reported ever serving on a federal riding executive and they were more likely to have been a federal candidate or to have worked on a federal election campaign. It seems likely then that these realists stay active in provincial politics largely as an offshoot of their federal partisan activity.

FEDERAL ACTIVISTS IN PROVINCIAL POLITICS

We expected that a comparison of the optimists and realists in our sample would find the former more active in the provincial party and responsible for its ability to maintain at least a nominal presence in British Columbia politics. But this is not so. An analysis of the level of activity by the degree of optimism suggests an inverse relationship: as the level of optimism increases, the degree of party participation decreases. Realists are more likely to have served on the provincial executive or on a provincial constituency executive, they are more likely to have been a provincial candidate and to have worked for a candidate, and to have worked for the party in the last provincial election.

And federal activism is inversely related to the level of optimism in provincial politics. As the degree of federal Liberal involvement increases the level of optimism about the provincial party's future decreases! But of the delegates to the provincial leadership selection convention, realists were significantly more likely to be federal constituency representatives, optimists were more likely to be provincial constituency representatives. We think that the federal constituency associations are less ephemeral than those organized for provincial ridings. All this can only reinforce our conclusion that the most significant provincial party activity is probably driven more by federal party activity than any genuine optimism about provincial politics.

CONCLUSION

This analysis of the Liberal party must be kept in perspective. The party remains a marginal player in the provincial party system and it consumes the energies of relatively few activists. But the fact that this many hardheaded partisans feel obliged, by virtue of their federal party loyalties, to sustain a provincial party testifies to the power of the Liberals to integrate the federal and provincial political worlds of many of their activists even if they can no longer do it for their electorate. It is also evidence of the power of Canadian Liberalism's commitment to the political centre and its abhorrence of a politics of polarization.

Here also may be a partial answer to our question as to why there are so few federal Liberals amongst Social Credit activists. It seems plausible that the character of their federal partisan commitments makes it particularly difficult for them to work in another party. Given that both the national Liberals and the provincial Socreds have been the governing party in their respective jurisdictions for most of the recent period, the conflicts between the two would have been especially difficult. This in turn would reinforce the Conservative cast to Social Credit making it less attractive to centrist Liberals. To explore these questions adequately we would need a good study of those federal Liberal activists who choose to play no part in provincial party life.

But this hardly resolves the puzzles of the Liberal party's survival in British Columbia's politics. Many of the arguments we have made would appear to hold, mutatis mutandis, for the provincial Conservatives. Yet federal Progressive Conservatives do not feel the need to try to maintain even a nominal organizational presence in provincial party competition. Is there some important difference here between the activists of the two national parties with the more nationalistic Liberals committed to a presence in all parts of the country? (After all, this same pattern characterizes Quebec.) Or is it simply a consequence of the disintegration of Conservative politics in British Columbia in the 1950s? As we noted in Chapter 1, the Conservatives were far more rapidly folded into Social Credit than were most Liberals. A fuller exploration of that decade might go a long way to explaining contemporary party organizations. Certainly some scholars have implied that the provincial Tory activists felt they were cast adrift by their federal counterparts (Black 1979b).

CHAPTER TEN

Towards the Centre?: The Dynamics of Two-Party Competition

BIPOLAR POLITICS AND CENTRISM

Polarized two-party systems provide the simplest form of political competition in electoral democracies. Each of the two parties offers the electorate a clear set of policy orientations and issue positions and the party closest to the preferences of the voting majority wins. Such straightforward models lie at the heart of some of the most persuasive accounts of electoral competition we have.

Electoral competition provides the dynamic force that stimulates change in parties' ideological orientations, policy positions, and organizations. In his influential book, *An Economic Theory of Democracy*, Anthony Downs (1957) argued that simple two-party competition would inevitably lead the parties to locate themselves immediately adjacent to one another at the centre. Not to do so would be irrational for a power-seeking party as it would guarantee victory to a more centrist opponent and condemn it to permanent electoral minority status.

Downs' argument focuses on the issue positions parties ought to take as a consequence of their competitive situation. Kirchheimer (1966) pushed this analysis of party systems considerably further by demonstrating the organizational consequences of this logic. He pointed out that modern cadre parties, which he labeled catch-all parties, were inherently better organized than mass parties to make the necessary (Downsian) policy adjustments. As a consequence (left-wing) mass parties had either to adopt many of the forms and mores of their (conservative) catch-all opponents or suffer long-term decline and continuing electoral defeat. His conclusion, based on a detailed study of the German Social Democrats, was that these structural imperatives spelled the end for ideologically-focused mass parties and heralded the transformation of western politics.

But electoral market incentives are not the only forces working on political parties for many elements of mass parties have been notoriously slow to disappear. David Butler (1960) suggested an important reason why this should be so in an essay which pointed to the competing balance of perspectives among voters, politicians, and organization activists within a party. He argued that party activists were everywhere more ideological, and therefore less accommodating, than were elected politicians, who in turn were themselves more ideological than their party's electoral supporters taken as a whole. This, he implies, is true for both mass parties of the left and catch-all parties of the right. But while party activists of both persuasions may be more extreme than their leaders and voters, because of the ideological and organizational traditions of mass parties, activists of the left are more resistant to the pressures of a Downsian slide to Kirchheimer's centrist party politics than those on the right. Seemingly, much of the history of the post-World War II British Labour party could be written in such terms.

This formulation leads our attention away from voters on the one hand, and politicians on the other, and back towards the pivotal role of party activists in ordering or limiting the extent or direction of change in a party system. They are central to a party's appeal for electoral support and can be an important force in shaping policy and directing leadership. By working on campaigns, and in sustaining party organizations between elections, they contribute to the magnitude, reach, and structure of voter support. They can expand or limit a party's success by their influence in choosing party candidates and leaders who are important to a party's popularity. As we have noted in Chapter 8, this was very much on the minds of Social Credit activists as they decided to select Bill Vander Zalm as their party leader, making a deliberate choice to return to a more populist politics. Activists also take positions on public policies and party issues, passing resolutions in party forums, and conventions which define the party's public face. New Democratic conventions have been known for this, adopting positions their more vote-conscious politicians would prefer never saw the light of day. Perhaps the best known of these was the national party's long-standing pledge to abandon NATO. But whether it is the choice of a controversial candidate or leader, or the assertion of some policy, all such decision-making by party activists constrains the struggle for competitive advantage in the wider system. Thus as activists limit a party's manoeuverability, party success may ultimately be related to the

congruence of opinion between its activists and the wider electorate.

Convincing as these arguments might be, they have rarely been
systematically tested. The BC party system provides an ideal case for
such a test. It has a system of two-party polarized competition that
has had a catch-all party of the right facing a mass party of the left.
According to Downs and Kirchheimer, the two ought to have come
to mirror one another. But they have not. We believe that the explanation for this can be found, as Butler suggested, in the differing
ideological character of their party activists. We also want to go on
to argue from there that the competitiveness of each of the two
principal parties is related to their ideological makeup, and its fit
with the province's political culture.

Though not exclusively ideological, party competition in British
Columbia has a sharper left/right focus than in any other part of
English-speaking North America. Federal institutions have allowed
the province's electoral competition to become detached from the
main currents of Canada's national politics which has focused on the
attempts of the old-line federal parties to broker a host of competing
regional, cultural, and socio-economic interests. The evolution of
party competition in British Columbia confirms the logic of both
Downs and Kirchheimer but it also demonstrates that there are limits to the processes of transformation.

Remember that the contemporary version of British Columbia's
polarized party system was born in 1952 with the collapse of a
wartime provincial coalition of Liberals and Conservatives. Though
Social Credit soon established an electoral dominance, it did not
initially absorb all the anti-socialist forces. The Conservatives
quickly disappeared into the new party but the Liberals managed to
hold onto about 20 per cent of the vote and a handful of seats. In
1972 the NDP won an election, but with only 39 per cent of the vote,
when much of the support of the aging Social Credit government
splintered and defected. It was reactions to that election which led
to the renewal of Social Credit leadership, the creation of a more
modern party organization, and the re-establishment of a new, more
complete Social Credit electoral coalition. In that rebuilding, Social
Credit finally managed to absorb most of the Liberal elites who had
resisted them for two decades. The next election returned Social
Credit to power and completed the creation of the modern bipolar
party system.

Although the Social Credit party attracted many Liberal notables
as it moved towards the centre for the 1975 election, it was not the
sole benefactor of the Liberal electoral collapse. Many former Liberal

voters turned to the NDP, responding to a general rightward drift towards the centre by the social democrats. Middle-class support for the NDP became especially evident among those with a university education as NDP policies appealed to the growing numbers of public sector professionals and others in occupations linked to the social policy net. A growing public sector electorate, increased middle-class support and the geographic spread of the working class strengthened the NDP. As a consequence, differences in the support levels of the two parties declined considerably as they came to split, almost evenly, the popular vote. This was true notwithstanding the fact that the plurality electoral system continued to return Social Credit governments. Thus, in the five elections from 1956 to 1969, the average vote spread between the two parties was 12 percentage points; but, in the three since 1975, this narrowed to 5 points with the two parties now taking nearly 93 per cent of the vote (Figure 1).

This apparent Downsian convergence towards balance at the centre did not go completely unchecked. While British Columbia has traditionally had a polarized political style, many of the differences were as much rhetorical as real. But in 1983, in the aftermath of another Social Credit electoral victory, the government launched a controversial and highly divisive package of neo-conservative policies. This sudden and dramatic set of changes had not been anticipated and was seen as an attack on the existing social contract. A massive public outcry revealed the danger of moving too far from the centre in a two-party system. Bennett, the principal architect of this system, who had been heard to describe his Social Credit as 'slightly right of centre' and the opposition New Democrats as 'slightly left of centre,' paid the political price of his party leadership over his miscalculation. As we noted in Chapter 8, the contestants for his job sought to distance themselves from these initiatives and Vander Zalm won because the delegates thought his populist style would appeal to confrontation-hating centrists.

Although the NDP and Social Credit clearly represented the polarities of mass and cadre organizational types in their formative years, party organization also changed as the system developed. At its founding, the CCF/NDP was a classic mass party. It was the creation of left-wing organizations, with roots outside the legislative arena, which formed a political party to achieve the goals of a movement which they believed were incompatible with those of the traditional parties. Individual members were at the core of the party's organization and controlled its structure and policy. Membership fees and small contributions financed its activity and political education was seen as one of its primary missions. The party's election campaigns depended on committed activists who worked at the grass roots soliciting support for the local candidates.

The organizational beginnings of the Social Credit party are more ambiguous and less well documented than those of the CCF. The original Social Credit League was a tiny fringe group which adhered to an unconventional monetary doctrine and its organizational characteristics were probably more like those of a social movement with an emphasis on the role and active participation of individual members than a typical bourgeois party. But after its quite unexpected victory in 1952, and the subsequent explosive growth under W.A.C. Bennett's leadership, the party quickly took on all the characteristics of a cadre party – a weak organizational structure dominated by its parliamentary leadership with little apparent interest in ongoing political education or extra-parliamentary activity. There is no systematic evidence about the social composition of the party's organization during this period, but it seems to have incorporated elements of the original group's base in an unsophisticated, largely rural or hinterland population suspicious of modern elites and government in general. The party appears to have had a populist style without the participatory features of a mass party: it existed to win elections for its conservative notables.

However, with the Social Credit defeat in 1972, part of the organizational renewal that resurrected the party to its former competitive status involved a major membership drive and an emphasis on the role of volunteer party members in party activity and election campaigns. The socialists, on the other hand, had already begun to undergo some of the transformation Kirchheimer predicted was necessary for mass parties to prosper. Their concern for political education, the means to 'the intellectual and moral encadrement of the masses' (1966:184), waned as they deradicalized and directed more attention to immediate electoral success. Moreover, as the revitalized Social Credit increasingly turned to more sophisticated campaign technologies, the NDP organization found itself attempting to meld its traditional grass roots approach with the imperatives of opinion polling and professionally managed modern electronic advertising techniques. As we saw in Chapter 3, this coincided with an increase in the number of middle-class professionals among activists in the NDP and some decline in the distinctiveness of the social profiles of the three parties.

Yet even with this recent convergence in the parties' organizational and personal characteristics, aspects of the earlier mass/cadre differences remain evident. The NDP membership tends to be seen as more active between elections, and its biennial party conventions appear to represent a more significant constraint on the options of the party leadership than is true in Social Credit. For example, the NDP constitution states that the leader is chief party spokesperson and as such is subject to the authority of the convention. The Social Credit constitution is silent on this relationship. Moreover, unlike the Social Credit party which allows its members to join other parties at the national level, the NDP restricts its membership to those who are willing to commit themselves exclusively to the NDP nationally as well as provincially.

PUTTING THE BRAKES ON CENTRISM

How can we explain the limits to convergence and to balance that appear to be at work in a party system that otherwise is behaving as Downs and Kirchheimer suggest? From Butler's argument, and our own view of the central importance that party activists play in shaping competitive behaviour, we expected to find the constraints embedded in the distribution of opinions held by the working core of the party.

In the British Columbia case, this led us to hypothesize that the views of NDP and Social Credit party activists would be distinctly different, and while there may be some overlap of opinion on some issues, of both style and substance, the number of these issues would be quite limited. Thus the nature and the extent of ideological flexibility within the parties, and the degree of overlap between them, should help us to identify the limits to further transformation in this polarized system.

We also expected to find important differences in both the structure of beliefs and the focus of activity between the left and the right. In particular, we expected that NDP party activists would be more homogeneous in their political and policy views than are their counterparts in the Social Credit Party, and that they would continue to be more concerned with party policy while Social Credit activists would be oriented to immediate electoral success.

To the extent this pattern holds, the NDP leadership should be more constrained by its membership and their views, and so less responsive to shifting public opinion. Taken together with the Social Credit party's record of continuing electoral success this leads us to infer that, in general the views of Social Credit activists are more consistent with those of the British Columbia electorate than are those of the NDP's militants. However, since the electoral position of the NDP is clearly a highly competitive one we also expect that, on some issues, the NDP more closely approximates popular views.

These propositions about the parameters which govern party adaptability can be explored with our data from the Social Credit and NDP activist surveys. In order to compare the opinions of these party activists with those of the wider electorate we also have the results of a survey undertaken in conjunction with a provincial election in 1979 (Blake 1985), several of whose measures were replicated in the leadership convention surveys. Although the survey of the electorate was undertaken some years before our delegate surveys, recent evidence suggests that on the general issues we address, opinion in British Columbia has not shifted in a significant way. For example, three of the items used to create the collective versus individual responsibility scales and which appear in Table 32 below were included in quarterly surveys by United Communications Research between November 1987 and January 1989. The distribution of opinion they found is very similar to that in the 1979 survey. Thus, while our comparisons must remain tentative because of the time differences between the various surveys, there is good reason for us to be confident about our basic findings.

To examine the distribution of opinion between the parties, and the comparative homogeneity with each, we used the responses to our comprehensive series of questions concerning two major dimensions of government activity: first, appropriate areas and levels of public spending, and, second, targets for regulation/deregulation. These are issues that became highly salient during the neo-conservative program undertaken by the Social Credit government, and ones that have clearly and publicly divided the parties since that time.

Our respondents divided predictably on both sets of issues (see Figures 4 and 5 above). The New Democrats are strongly in favour of both increased government spending and public regulation in most areas while the Social Credit partisans preferred existing or decreased levels of spending on most programs and the same or lower levels of regulation in all areas. More particularly given our concerns here, the comparative homogeneity of the mass party on the left is readily evident. In a majority of areas the NDP respondents were both highly agreed on the general direction government policy should take and presented a more coherent front than their Social Credit counterparts. On only three of the sixteen items – spending on tourism and highways and the regulation of gambling – were they the less homogeneous of the two parties. None of these issues seems particularly salient to their traditional ideological perspective or issue agenda.

Chapter 6 makes it clear that while there is some overlap in party opinion on government spending the extent of the congruence is very limited. Where it exists it comes primarily from issues that are most obviously linked to economic development (tourism, highways, and reforestation). This reflects a common interest in developmental policies of the sort often shared by the left and the right and indeed by most Canadian provincial governments. In British Columbia, given its geography and resources, this has traditionally been found in government support for the forest industry (most of the forest resource is owned by the state) and more recently for a government role in expanding tourism.

Opinion on regulation/deregulation targets does seem to suggest rather more overlap between the two parties but that is largely due to Social Credit being spread more evenly across the spectrum. The governing right is very heterogeneous in these matters: for instance policy disagreements over the marketing of agricultural products reflect a rural/urban split in Social Credit. The NDP remains as agreed on regulation questions as it was on public spending. The areas of greatest party overlap (as measured by average party difference scores on each item) are those that involve conventional (Canadian) moral issues such as the consumption of alcohol, gambling, and Sunday shopping. On those it is the NDP that has shifted ground, moving closer to the Socreds to support the status quo or a decrease in regulation.

Whatever policy convergence there may be between the parties as they compete for electoral support, the party activists continue to carry quite distinct and largely opposed policy preferences and orientations. True to its heritage as a party of mass integration, the NDP is more coherent; its key activists' preferences appear more constrained and disciplined by a predictable world view. This leads us to the matter of whether these partisans also have different attitudes towards party activity and electoral strategy.

The question of the relative importance of electoral success versus maintaining the integrity of party policy is obviously a delicate one for party activists. Being concerned with electoral success regardless of policy is presumably not an image many partisans would like to see identified with their party. As a consequence our two questions only indirectly address this trade-off. One of these is concerned with policy directions each party might take; the other is focused on modern pragmatic electoral methods generally.

With respect to policy direction, we assume that party activists, for whom electoral success is the primary preoccupation, will be loathe to see their party move too far from the political centre. For Social Credit this explicitly Downsian notion translates into concern

that the party will move too far to the right; for the NDP it would be a
worry they might turn too far to the left. On the more narrow practi-
cal question of electoral tactics we assume that those who are essentially more interested in substantive policy matters than in immediate electoral success would be comparatively unhappy with the
growing emphasis on advertising and public opinion polling in contemporary politics. Activists motivated by ideology fear the capacity
of polls to tempt and contaminate their party's policy stances.

Although only rough indicators of the primacy party activists
accord electoral success, responses to the questions about polling
and the dangers of extremism do support our hypothesis. The differences are not large but they are in the expected directions (Table 31).
In both parties, opinion polls and advertising are clearly unpopular,
though in Social Credit's case this seems to flow from the populist
orientations (discussed below) of many of its militants. The two
were significantly related among Social Crediters, but not among
New Democrats. Over half of the Socreds believe that their party has
to be careful not to move too far to the right but only 44 per cent of
the NDP agree that they need to avoid moving too far to the left.
What does seem to differentiate the two is the nature of the opposition in each party to the moderate course. The NDP appears more
polarized on this issue of the appropriateness of an ideological politics; Socreds are much less evenly split.

TABLE 31
Activists' orientations to electoral success
(vertical percentages)

	Social Credit	NDP
The party has to be careful not to move too far to the (left/right):		
agree	54.8	44.1
disagree	35.2	50.1
no opinion	10.0	5.8
	(330)	(365)
There is too much emphasis on public opinion polls and slick advertising in politics today:		
agree	66.7	74.4
disagree	25.5	22.3
no opinion	7.9	3.4
	(330)	(368)

Finally, two different sets of measures were available from the surveys of both the activists and the electorate to test our expectations about the distance between activist and popular opinion. These are the measures of collectivist/individualist orientations and populism which have had particular relevance for the content and style of party competition in the province. The first, which most closely parallels the party conflicts over social planning and government intervention versus free market competition, is said to divide ordinary British Columbians; the second, which structures the approach to politics, has been shown to unite them (Blake 1985).

Scale scores on the individualism/collectivism measure once again illustrate an unambiguously bipolar distribution of opinion between the parties and the more homogeneous cast of NDP militants as compared to Social Credit (Table 32). They also substantiate our hypothesis that Social Credit opinion is closer to that of the electorate than is that in the NDP: the mean scores for the Social Credit militants is 3.7, for the NDP just 0.4, and for the general electorate 2.4. However, it should be noted that, as we anticipated, on some of the separate items the NDP seems more in tune with popular opinion than the overall scores might suggest. For instance, on standard of living guarantees the NDP is clearly closer to the public than is Social Credit, the public falls between the parties (though on the NDP side) with respect to old age pensions, and there is unanimity among British Columbians, partisans and electorate alike, about the need for public health care. Here is support for our prediction, rooted in continuing Social Credit victories, that, generally speaking, the contemporary balance of opinion among activists is tilted in Social Credit's favour.

On our measures of populism, the Social Credit camp, with its populist traditions, seems even more in tune with public opinion (Table 33). The comparative means are 2.2 for the electorate, 2.3 for Social Credit activists, and only 1.4 for NDP activists. But the NDP also has its populist elements as indicated by the lack of agreement within the party on these issues. Compared to most of our other questions, on these the NDP shows a striking diversity of opinion. This suggests some tension between its traditions of grassroots activism on the one hand, and the professional and academic orientations of many of its contemporary activists on the other. Indeed, the New Democrats may actually be increasing their divergence from the electorate on this strand in the popular culture. Populism is negatively related to education among NDP activists and, as we noted in Chapter 3, increases in the educational levels of activists is one of the most dramatic changes to have marked the party in the last decade and a half. The extent of this ambivalence is further indicated

TABLE 32
Collectivism/individualism: activists and the electorate
(per cent agreeing with individualist response)

	Electorate	Socred activists	NDP activists
The government ought to make sure that everyone has a decent standard of living	19.6	70.3	2.4
Let's face it, most unemployed people could find a job if they really wanted to	58.7	54.9	2.2
Why should the government spend my tax money on sick people; my family always put aside something for a rainy day	7.5	6.0	0.5
After a person has worked until 65, it is proper for the community to support him or her	38.5	64.8	12.3
Government regulation stifles personal initiative OR Without government regulations, some people would just take advantage of the rest of us	75.1	68.3	2.2
If I do my best, it is only right that the government should help me out when I get some bad breaks OR Each individual should accept the consequences of their own actions	63.0	94.5	20.2
Mean collectivism/individualism scale scores	2.43	3.74	.39

NOTE: Respondents were asked to choose the item in each set of paired statements which came closest to their own viewpoint. The other statements were agree/disagree items.

by the uncharacteristically high percentage of NDP respondents (40%) who said they had no opinion, refused to answer, or provided their own set of categories for one or other of these populism questions.

THE DYNAMICS OF ELECTORAL COMPETITION IN BC

Despite general Downsian centripetal forces, and gradual organizational imitation, party activists in British Columbia continue to artic-

TABLE 33
Populism: activists and the electorate
(per cent agreeing with populist response)

	Electorate	Socred activists	NDP activists
In the long run, I'll place my trust in the simple, down-to-earth thinking of ordinary people rather than the theories of experts and intellectuals	60.6	61.0	31.6
We could probably solve most of our big political problems if government could actually be brought back to people at the grassroots	73.8	57.2	48.0
What we need is a government that gets the job done without all this red tape	88.7	90.2	37.0
Populism scale mean scores	2.24	2.34	1.36

NOTE: All questions asked the respondents to indicate if they agreed, disagreed or had no opinion about each statement.

ulate divergent and opposed views. Clearly there are substantial limits to convergence. Indeed, as Butler argued, party militants are likely to be one of the major factors in constraining two-party convergence and the triumph of the centre. The continuing ideological rhetoric of British Columbia politics appears to have important roots in the culture of its parties' activists.

As we expected, despite its transformation, the New Democratic mass party of the left is characterized by a set of activists who are more concerned with policy purity, and more homogeneous in their views, than is its more obviously catch-all opponent. This plus the party's organizational traditions give the NDP's leadership less opportunity to move easily in response to public opinion and less flexibility in the range of policy positions they might adopt. On balance this must put the NDP at an inherent comparative electoral disadvantage when faced by a party whose apparent raison d'être, defeating socialism, is testimony to political opportunism.

As an organizationally modernized cadre party, Social Credit is in a strong position. Not only do its activists make winning elections their first (some say only) priority, they hold divergent enough views that the party's leadership can always choose from a wide range of positions and find some support for their decision among party activists. It is also this divergence that tends to produce the greater congruence between the catch-all party and popular opinion. On occasion, however, this strategy has missed the mark. Bill Bennett's restraint program and Bill Vander Zalm's privatization initiatives both alienated large sectors of the public even though they were popular with the party's right wing.

Though the *form* of an electorally bipolar system has emerged as Downs and Kirchheimer predicted, the underlying party cultures do not provide for balanced competition. Social Credit is less constrained, hence more capable of assuming popular positions, and so continues in office. And there may be some reason to think that in this situation a 'minority party syndrome' will work to maintain this equilibrium (Perlin 1980). Without the perquisites of power to reward its supporters (either in terms of policy or more tangible personal rewards) the NDP is less attractive to pragmatists. This only reinforces the ideological cast of its cadre of activists, which in turn attracts more purists, and perpetuates the system.

The evidence does show that party/electorate policy congruence varies by issue and that in some areas the NDP has the advantage. This helps to explain why, though it occupies a more restricted ideological space, the NDP has been able to increase its vote and to challenge Social Credit. When the political agenda turns to matters such as support for seniors or concern for the unemployed then the NDP has an advantage. This may also be true for environmental issues as public views appear to be shifting in the direction of NDP opinion. Moreover, the experience of the 1986 defeat, when the party was so close to success yet was defeated by a classic brokerage appeal to leadership image, convinced NDP activists to endorse a leader whose style is determinedly moderate.

Social Credit would seem to have its most marked advantage in non-ideological terms for the populist orientations of its militants provide a much closer fit with the electorate than do those of the NDP. It is ironic that in an ideologically polarized politics questions of style could provide a greater competitive advantage than those of substance. But even here the results are equivocal for the populist orientations of Social Credit militants may work to limit the party's leadership in their efforts to build a sophisticated (Kirchheimerian) organization. As we noted in previous chapters, populist predispositions significantly reduce Social Credit activists' acceptance of professional polling and advertising, and the leadership convention which chose Vander Zalm saw the populists among Social Credit turn their back on a modern organizational style of party and leadership.

Downs and Kirchheimer provide models of two-party competition that account for much of the change and evolution of such systems. But as Butler noted, voters and vote-seeking politicians are not the only actors who drive electoral politics. Party activists constitute the working core of any political party: their attitudes and organizational preferences influence competitive practice, constrain party options and movement, and appear to constitute a set of limits to party convergence. As the British Columbia case illustrates, party activists do carry distinctive political subcultures and these may have a significant impact on the ongoing dynamics and immediate outcomes in competitive party systems.

Appendix

The attitude scales utilized in this analysis were derived from a large battery of 'agree/disagree' items plus Likert-type items measuring degree of support for spending increases or decreases in a variety of policy areas and degree of support for increases or decreases in government regulation. Some scales are identical to those used in previous analyses of federal party activists (Blake 1988) or provincial voters (Blake 1985).

The items used to construct each scale are given below. For 'agree/disagree' items, the answer corresponding to the direction in which the scale is scored appears in parentheses. Where a scale item is based on the choice between a pair of statements, the choice corresponding to the direction of the scale is indicated. Those responding in the direction in which the scale was scored for a given item were given a score of 1, 0 otherwise. The total scale score for a respondent is the sum of these item scores. The category combinations corresponding to the direction in which the scale was scored are given in parentheses. Further details of scale construction are available on request.

ATTITUDE SCALES: ALL RESPONDENTS

Collective versus Individual Responsibility
(scale scored in individual responsibility direction)

1 After a person has worked until 65, it is proper for the community to support him or her. (Disagree)
2 The government ought to make sure that everyone has a decent standard of living. (Disagree)
3 Let's face it, most unemployed people could find a job if they really wanted to. (Agree)
4 Why should the government spend my tax dollars on sick people; my family

always put aside something for a rainy day. (Agree)

5 Government regulation stifles personal initiative. OR Without government regulation, some people will just take advantage of the rest of us. (Chose first statement)

6 If I do my best, it is only right that the government should help me out when I get some bad breaks. OR Each individual should accept the consequences of their own actions. (Chose second statement)

Populism
(scale scored in populist direction)

1 In the long run, I'll put my trust in the simple, down-to-earth thinking of ordinary people rather than the theories of experts and intellectuals. (Agree)

2 We would probably solve most of our big national problems if government could actually be brought back to the people at the grass roots. (Agree)

3 What we need is government that gets the job done without all this red tape. (Agree)

Continentalism
(scored in continentalist direction)

1 Canada should have freer trade with the United States. (Agree)

2 Canada's independence is threatened by the large percentage of foreign ownership in key sectors of our economy. (Disagree)

3 We must ensure an independent Canada even if that were to mean a lower standard of living for Canadians. (Disagree)

Antiregulation
(scored in anti-regulation direction)

This scale was created by assigning a score from –2 to +2 to respondents depending on whether they believed that government regulation should be substantially reduced (2), slightly reduced (1), kept as now (0), slightly extended (–1), or substantially extended (–2). The scores were then summed across seven policy areas then divided by seven to return to the original measurement range. The policy areas were: environmental protection, marketing of agricultural products, land use, sale of alcohol, shopping hours, and gambling.

Government Spending Scale
(scored in pro-spending direction)

This scale was created by assigning a score from –2 to +2 to respondents depending on whether they believed that government spending should be substantially reduced (–2), slightly reduced (–1), kept as now (0), slightly extended (+1), or substantially extended (+2). The scores were then summed across seven policy areas then divided by seven to return to the original measurement range. The policy areas were: education, welfare rates, health care, reforestation, job creation grants, highways, tourism, public service salaries, and daycare.

ATTITUDE SCALES: SOCIAL CREDIT ACTIVISTS

Social Spending
(scored in pro-spending direction)

This scale was created by assigning a score from -2 to +2 to respondents depending on whether they believed that government spending in social policy areas should be substantially increased (2), slightly increased (1), kept as now (0), slightly reduced (-1), or substantially reduced (-2). The scores were then summed across four policy areas then divided by four to return to the original measurement range. The policy areas were: education, welfare rates, health care, and daycare.

Restraint
(scale scored in pro-restraint direction)

1 The size of government in BC should be reduced even if this means a lower level of public services. (Agree)
2 There should be a law requiring the government to balance the provincial budget. (Agree)
3 Government spending on public service salaries should be (slightly or substantially decreased).
4 Regulation of human rights should be (slightly or substantially reduced).
5 Government spending on education should be (slightly or substantially decreased).
6 Government spending on welfare rates should be (slightly or substantially decreased).
7 The restraint program was well intentioned but not well implemented. OR Opponents of the restraint program just could not accept losing the 1983 election. (Chose second statement)

ATTITUDE SCALES: NDP ACTIVISTS

Lifestyle Regulation
(scored in anti-regulation direction)

The procedure followed was identical to that used for constructing the anti-regulation scale except that it was based only on the sale of alcohol, shopping hours and gambling policy areas. This scale was used only for analysis of NDP activists.

Public Ownership
(scored in pro-public ownership direction)

This scale ranges from 0 to 12 depending on how many from a set of corporations – some publicly owned, others privately owned – for which public
ownership was favoured. The six corporations were: BC Place, Whistler Corporation, MacMillan Bloedel, Quintette Mines, the Bank of BC, and BC Telephone. For a given corporation, respondents were assigned a score of 2 if
they favoured complete public ownership, 1 if they favoured partial public
ownership, and 0 if they favoured complete private ownership. The scores
were then summed across corporations for each respondent.

Downsize
(scored in pro-downsizing direction)

1 Social security programs (like old age pensions and family allowances)
should be based on family income needs, and people who don't need this
type of assistance should not receive it. (Disagree)
2 The size of government in BC should be maintained even if this means an
increase in taxes. (Agree)

Strike Restriction
(scored in anti-restriction direction)

Respondents were assigned a score from 0 to 8 depending on the extent of
restriction on the right to strike they would favour for nurses, police, hospital workers, and firefighters. For each occupation, those favouring no
restrictions received a score of 0, those favouring some restrictions a score of
1, and those favouring no right to strike a score of 2.

POLICY ITEMS

A large number of agree/disagree and forced choice items were utilized to
assess intra-party consensus. Some of them were also used in constructing
the scales described above. The exact wording of the items used in the
analysis of consensus is as follows.

A. ALL ACTIVISTS

1 The government ought to make sure that everyone has a decent standard
of living.
2 In the long run, I'll put my trust in the simple down-to-earth thinking of
ordinary people rather than the theories of experts and intellectuals.
3 Let's face it, most unemployed people could find a job if they really
wanted to.

4 We could probably solve most of our big political problems if government could actually be brought back to people at the grass roots.

5 Why should the government spend my tax money on sick people; my family always put aside something for a rainy day.

6 What we need is a government that gets the job done without all this red tape.

7 After a person has worked until 65, it is proper for the community to support him or her.

8 Canada should have freer trade with the United States.

9 Trade unions have too much power in British Columbia.

10 We must ensure an independent Canada even if that were to mean a lower standard of living for Canadians.

11 BC companies should be given preference for provincial government contracts even if the cost is higher.

12 The provincial government should negotiate with the province's native population on land claims.

13 Canada's independence is threatened by the large percentage of foreign ownership in key sectors of the economy.

14 There should be a law requiring the government to balance the provincial budget.

15 Governments should make a concerted effort to improve the social and economic position of women. OR Women should help themselves and should not expect governments to make special efforts on their behalf.

16 Government regulation stifles personal initiative. OR Without government regulations, some people would just take advantage of the rest of us.

B. NDP AND LIBERAL ACTIVISTS

1 A free trade agreement with the United States would inevitably lead to restrictions on the rights of workers in Canada.

2 Social security programs (like old age pensions and family allowances) should be based on family income needs, and people who don't need this type of assistance should not receive it.

3 The government ought to make sure that everyone who wants to work can find a job.

4 The size of government should be maintained even if this means an increase in taxes.

5 One of the main reasons for poverty is that the economy is based on private ownership and profits.

6 Big corporations have so much power that we also need big unions.

7 Trade unions should be required to conduct a secret ballot before authorizing strike action.

8 Public sector workers have a lot more job security than private sector workers.
9 During a strike, management should not be allowed to hire workers to take the place of strikers.

C. LIBERAL ACTIVISTS

1 The Senate of Canada should be elected.
2 Do you believe that people in the various provinces should put less emphasis on their distinctive regional identities and more emphasis on their common Canadian identity?
3 In relation to other provinces, do you feel that British Columbia has received equitable treatment from the federal government?
  Liberal activists were also asked whether they agreed or disagreed with the BC government's position on the following issues: privatization, the Meech Lake Accord, the Canada-U.S. Free Trade Agreement, and decentralization of government services; whether they approved or disapproved of 'the present policy for making the federal public service bilingual' and 'the principle of official bilingualism'; and whether they were 'personally in favour of the Meech Lake agreement to amend the Canadian constitution.'

Notes

CHAPTER 1: THE POLARIZATION OF BC POLITICS

1 Even 33,000 was larger than the NDP membership figure at the time – 28,368. See Allan Whitehorn (1988:273)

CHAPTER 4: SOCIAL CREDIT

1 The consensus index equals the absolute value of 50 minus the percentage agreeing with a given statement.

2 Data from these leadership convention studies were made available by George Perlin of Queen's University. Professor Perlin bears no responsibility for the use made of these data in this book.

3 This factor analysis procedure is similar to that used by Richard Johnston in his analysis of the structure of beliefs within the federal Liberal and Conservative parties. He argues that using correlations between pairs of policy items to measure the degree of constraint, as Converse (1964) does, underestimates the degree of ideological constraint in a group. See Johnston (1988:58–60) for a detailed rationale and further explanation of the technique.

4 Principal components analysis with varimax rotation was the technique used. While the number of factors extracted after rotation differed by activist group, the continentalism items had their highest loadings on the second factor for all groups except BC Socreds where they loaded on the third factor.

CHAPTER 5: THE NEW DEMOCRATS

1 Keith Archer and Alan Whitehorn kindly made these data available to us.

For a description of the survey and a larger account of its results see Archer and Whitehorn (1988). They bear no responsibility for the use of the data here.

2 Our measure of rural/urban delegates was necessarily crude given that we had no direct question on this: we simply divided our sample into those from Victoria and the Lower Mainland on one hand and those from outside these major urban regions on the other. The Tau-c correlation between this variable and support for increased regulation of agricultural marketing was $-.16$.

3 These conclusions are based on the results of varimax rotation which produced as its first factor this 'lifestyle' dimension. In a principle components analysis, the first factor produced was one which combined high loadings on these three lifestyle questions and a loading of $-.45$ on one populism item concerning government red tape.

4 On the basis of our evidence we cannot reject the argument that a number of these delegates considered that it was the *weakness* rather than the fact of union ties that brought electoral defeat. However, since we have no indication from comments on our questionnaire that this is how our item was interpreted, and given the climate of opinion concerning organized labour in Canada, we concluded it was not the weakness of such ties that was at issue.

5 The scores for women and men were 7.8 and 6.9 respectively. The difference was significant at 0.02.

CHAPTER 7: LEADERSHIP SELECTION IN THE BC PARTIES

1 There is a similar pattern in the NDP data, though in that case the relationship is not statistically significant.

2 For an account of this at the national level see the Martin, Gregg, and Perlin (1983) description of John Crosbie's creation of student organizations in Newfoundland during the 1983 Conservative leadership race.

CHAPTER 8: THE SOCIAL CREDIT GRASSROOTS

1 Only 15% of the delegates committed to one of the eight minor candidates said their commitment was binding after the first ballot. That compares to 60% of McCarthy, 59% of Bud Smith, 54% of Brian Smith, and 46% of Vander Zalm people.

2 Given that delegates still had six choices – a majority is a tough test. But even if we were to alter it to a plurality, the story would not change.

3 The following independent variables, in addition to those reported in Table 30, were tested: federal vote (an indicator of connections to the federal Tories), all the other attitude scales in Table 29, and a three-item

index combining items critical of 'machine' politics. None were significant in the regression equations.

CHAPTER 9: RESISTING POLARIZATION

1 Dove Hendren, President, *Executive Reports to the 1987 Convention*, 8, 9, 10 May, Richmond, BC.
2 Art Lee, *Liberal Insight: Leadership Convention 1987*, pamphlet, 4.
3 John Turner, letter to delegates, October 1987.
4 John Turner, letter to policy convention, May 1987.
5 John Turner, *Liberal Insight: Leadership Convention 1987*, pamphlet, 2.
6 Art Lee, letter to policy convention, May 1987.
7 John Turner, letter to leadership convention delegates, October 1987.

Bibliography

Abramowitz, Alan, John McGlennon, and Ronald B. Rapoport (1986). 'Incentives for Activism.' Rapoport, Ronald B., Alan I. Abramowitz, and John B. McGlennon, *The Life of the Parties: Activists in Presidential Politics*. Lexington: University of Kentucky Press

Allen, Robert and Gideon Rosenbluth, eds. (1986). *Restraining the Economy: Social Credit Economic Politics for BC in the Eighties*. Vancouver: New Star Books

Alper, Donald K. (1975). 'From Rule to Ruin: The Conservative Party of British Columbia, 1928–1954.' Unpublished PH.D. dissertation, University of British Columbia

Archer, Keith and Alan Whitehorn (1988). 'Opinion Structure among NDP Activists.' Presented to the Annual Meeting of the Canadian Political Science Association. Windsor, Ont.

Black, Edwin R. (1979a). 'British Columbia: The Politics of Exploitation.' Hugh Thorburn, ed., *Party Politics in Canada*, 4th ed. Scarborough, Ont.: Prentice-Hall

– (1979b). 'Federal Strains within a Canadian Party.' Hugh Thorburn, ed., *Party Politics in Canada*, 4th ed. Scarborough, Ont.: Prentice-Hall

Blake, Donald E. (1984). 'The Electoral Significance of Public Sector Bashing.' *BC Studies* 62:29–43

– (1985). *Two Political Worlds: Parties and Voting in British Columbia*. Vancouver: University of British Columbia Press

– (1988). 'Division and Cohesion: The Major Parties.' George Perlin, ed., *Party Democracy in Canada: The Politics of National Conventions*. Scarborough, Ont.: Prentice-Hall

–, R.K. Carty, and Lynda Erickson (1988). 'Ratification or Repudiation: Social Credit Leadership Selection in British Columbia.' *Canadian Journal of Political Science* 21:513–37

-, R.K. Carty, and Lynda Erickson (1989). 'Federalism, Conservatism and the Social Credit Party in BC.' *BC Studies* 81:3-23

-, Richard Johnston, and David J. Elkins (1981). 'Sources of Change in the BC Party System.' *BC Studies* 50:3-28

Butler, David (1960). 'The Paradox of Party Difference.' *American Behavioral Scientist* 4:3-5

Carty, R.K. (1988). 'Campaigning in the Trenches: The Transformation of Constituency Politics.' George Perlin, ed., *Party Democracy in Canada: The Politics of National Conventions*. Scarborough, Ont.: Prentice-Hall

-, Lynda Erickson, and Donald E. Blake, eds. (1991). *Leaders and Parties in Canadian Politics: The Experience of the Provinces*. Toronto: HBJHolt

Christian, William and Colin Campbell (1983). *Political Parties and Ideologies in Canada*. Toronto: McGraw-Hill Ryerson

Converse, Philip E. (1964). 'The Nature of Belief Systems in Mass Publics.' David Apter, ed., *Democracy and Discontent*. New York: Free Press

Courtney, John (1986). 'Leadership Conventions and the Development of the National Political Community in Canada.' R.K. Carty and W.P. Ward, eds., *National Politics and Community in Canada*. Vancouver: University of British Columbia Press

Dahl, Robert A. (1956). *A Preface to Democratic Theory*. Chicago: University of Chicago Press

Dobie, Edith (1980) [1938]. 'Party History in British Columbia, 1903-1933.' J. Friesen and K. Ralston, eds., *Historical Essays on British Columbia*. Toronto: Gage

Downs, Anthony (1957). *An Economic Theory of Democracy*. New York: Harper & Row

Elkins, David (1976). 'Politics Makes Strange Bedfellows: The BC Party System in the 1952 and 1953 Provincial Elections.' *BC Studies* 30:3-26

- (1985). 'British Columbia as a State of Mind.' Donald E. Blake, ed., *Two Political Worlds: Parties and Voting in British Columbia*. Vancouver: University of British Columbia Press

Harris, Christopher C. (1987). 'British Columbia 1972-1975: The Genesis of a Two-Party System.' Unpublished MA thesis, University of British Columbia

James, P.E. (1987). 'Canadian Provincial Premiers: A Statistical Analysis of 185 Careers.' Unpublished MA thesis, University of British Columbia

Johnston, Richard (1988). 'The Ideological Structure of Opinion on Policy.' George Perlin, ed., *Party Democracy in Canada: The Politics of National Conventions*. Scarborough, Ont.: Prentice-Hall

Kirchheimer, Otto (1966). 'The Transformation of the Western European Party Systems.' J. LaPalombara and M. Weiner, eds., *Political Parties and Political Development*. Princeton: Princeton University Press

Kristianson, G.L. (1977). 'The Non-Partisan Approach to BC Politics: The Search for a Unity Party, 1972-1975.' *BC Studies* 33:13-29

Laycock, David (1990). *Populism and Democratic Thought in the Canadian Prairies, 1910-1945*. Toronto: University of Toronto Press

Magnusson, Warren, William Carroll, Charles Doyle, Monika Langer, and R.B.J. Walker, eds. (1984). *The New Reality: The Politics of Restraint in British Columbia*. Vancouver: New Star Books

Martin, Patrick, Allan Gregg, and George Perlin (1983). *Contenders: The Tory Quest for Power*. Scarborough, Ont.: Prentice-Hall

McCormack, A. Ross (1974). 'The Emergence of the Socialist Movement in BC.' *BC Studies* 21:3-27

Mitchell, David J. (1983). *W.A.C.: Bennett and the Rise of British Columbia*. Vancouver: Douglas & McIntyre

Ornstein, Michael D. and H.M. Stevenson (1984). 'Ideology and Public Policy in Canada.' *British Journal of Political Science* 14:313-44

Palmer, Vaughan (1989a). 'Socred War Chest Running Low on Cash.' Vancouver *Sun*, 9 March

– (1989b). 'Socred Membership Appears to be Down.' Vancouver *Sun*, 10 March

Perlin, George (1980). *The Tory Syndrome: Leadership Politics in the Progressive Conservative Party*. Montreal: McGill-Queen's University Press

– ed. (1988). *Party Democracy in Canada: The Politics of National Party Conventions*. Scarborough, Ont.: Prentice-Hall

Rapoport, Ronald B., Alan I. Abramowitz, and John McGlennon (1986). *The Life of the Parties: Activists in Presidential Politics*. Lexington: University of Kentucky Press

Resnick, Philip (1977). 'Social Democracy in Power: The Case of British Columbia.' *BC Studies* 34:3-20

Robin, Martin (1973). *Pillars of Profit: The Company Province*. Toronto: McClelland & Stewart

Siegfried, André (1970) [1906]. *The Race Question in Canada*. Toronto: McClelland & Stewart

Simeon, Richard and E. Robert Miller (1979). 'Regional Variations in Public Policy.' David J. Elkins and Richard Simeon, eds., *Small Worlds: Provinces and Parties in Canadian Political Life*. Toronto: Methuen

Smiley, Donald V. (1962). 'Canada's Poujadists: A New Look at Social Credit.' *Canadian Forum* 43:121-3

So, Robyn (1988). 'Incentives for Activism in a Moribund Political Party: The Case of the BC Liberals.' Unpublished MA thesis, University of British Columbia

Sorauf, Frank J. (1964). *Political Parties in the American System*. Boston: Little, Brown and Co.

Stewart, Ian (1988). 'The Brass Versus the Grass: Party Insiders and Out-
    siders at Canadian Leadership Conventions.' George Perlin, ed., *Party
    Democracy in Canada: The Politics of National Party Conventions*. Scarborough,
    Ont.: Prentice-Hall
Tomblin, Stephen G. (1990). 'W.A.C. Bennett and Province-Building in Brit-
    ish Columbia.' *BC Studies* 85:45-61
Whitehorn, Alan (1988). 'The New Democratic Party in Convention.' George
    Perlin, ed., *Party Democracy in Canada: The Politics of National Party Conven-
    tions*. Scarborough, Ont.: Prentice-Hall
Young, Walter D. (1969). *The Anatomy of a Party: The National CCF, 1932-61*.
    Toronto: University of Toronto Press
- (1971). 'A Profile of Activists in the British Columbia NDP.' *Journal of Cana-
    dian Studies* 6:19-26
- (1978). *Democracy and Discontent*, 2d ed. Toronto: McGraw-Hill Ryerson
- (1981). 'Ideology, Personality and the Origin of the CCF in British Colum-
    bia.' W. Peter Ward and Robert A.J. McDonald, eds., *British Columbia: His-
    torical Readings*. Vancouver: Douglas & McIntyre
- (1983). 'Political Parties.' J.T. Morley, Norman J. Ruff, Neil A. Swainson, R.
    Jeremy Wilson, and Walter D. Young, eds., *The Reins of Power: Governing
    British Columbia*. Vancouver: Douglas & McIntyre

Index